Jimmy exploded! He threw his toy truck on the floor! This was the third time this week. He was restless at school, and he was waking up two or three times every night. His mother couldn't understand why he had changed so. She was sure he was happy—after all, they were getting settled in their new home and their new church. His dog died three weeks ago but they were even replacing him. Why was Jimmy like this?

You guessed it—stress.

Kids experience stress a great deal more than we want to believe—they have as many problems as adults do. In this book we will see how we can help our children and our teens handle their stress

Dr. H. Norman Wright has also written

Crisis Counseling

Published by Here's Life Publishers

H. NORMAN WRIGHT

Helping Your Kids Handle

STRESS

 Here's Life Publishers

First printing, October 1989

Published by
HERE'S LIFE PUBLISHERS, INC.
P. O. Box 1576
San Bernardino, CA 92402

Adapted from *Helping Teens Handle Stress* (© 1987) and *Helping Children Handle Stress* (© 1987), both by H. Norman Wright.

Printed in the United States of America, by Arcata Graphics/Kingsport, Kingsport, TN.

Library of Congress Cataloging-in-Publication Data
　　Wright, H. Norman.
　　　　Helping your kids handle stress / H. Norman Wright.

　　　　　　p.　　　cm.

　　　　ISBN 0-89840-271-9

　　　　1. Stress in children.　2. Stress management.
　　3. Child rearing—religious aspects—Christianity.
　　4. Children—Religious life.　5. Christian life—1960-
　　I. Title.
　　BF723.S75W765　　　1990
　　649'.1—dc20　　　　　　　　　　　　　89-27607
　　　　　　　　　　　　　　　　　　　　　　　CIP

Scripture quotations are from *The New American Standard Bible,* © The Lockman Foundation 1960, 1962, 1963, 1968, 1971, 1972, 1975, 1977.

For More Information, Write:
　L.I.F.E.—P.O. Box A399, Sydney South 2000, Australia
　Campus Crusade for Christ of Canada—Box 300, Vancouver, B.C., V6C 2X3, Canada
　Campus Crusade for Christ—Pearl Assurance House, 4 Temple Row, Birmingham, B2 5HG, England
　Lay Institute for Evangelism—P.O. Box 8786, Auckland 3, New Zealand
　Campus Crusade for Christ—P.O. Box 240, Raffles City Post Office, Singapore 9117
　Great Commission Movement of Nigeria—P.O. Box 500, Jos, Plateau State Nigeria, West Africa
　Campus Crusade for Christ International—Arrowhead Springs, San Bernardino, CA 92414, U.S.A.

CONTENTS

Bitter are the tears of a child:
Sweeten them.
Deep are the thoughts of a child:
Quiet them.
Soft is the heart of a child:
Do not harden it.
— *Lady Pamela Windham Glenconner*

¤¤¤ 1 ¤¤¤

THE WORLD OF KIDS

Jimmy exploded, and he threw his toy truck on the floor! This was the third time this week. He was restless at school, and he was waking up two or three times every night. His mother just couldn't understand why his behavior had changed so much. She was sure he was happy—after all, they were getting settled in their new home, and they finally had located a new church which would meet all their needs. This week they were even going to look for a new puppy to replace Jack, their collie who had died three weeks before. Why was Jimmy like this?

You guessed it—stress.

Kids experience stress a great deal more than we would like to believe. No matter what a child's age is, his world holds as many problems as an adult's. We may feel a child's stress is of less intensity or importance than that of an adult, but that is not necessarily true. Children's trials can be especially traumatic for them, and can produce tragic long-term results. Troubled children need help in handling stress, and the sooner we can give them that help, the better chance they will have to grow and develop into emotionally healthy and mature individuals. In this book we'll examine several aspects of stress that occur in childhood and during the teen years, and we will look at a number of things we can do to help our children cope with that stress.

Early Childhood—The "Magic Years"

Part of the process of understanding and helping a child handle stress is understanding how a child thinks and how he perceives life. Early childhood has been called the "magic years." The ages of three to six make up this time period. We call this the time of magical thinking because at this stage the child thinks he is omnipotent. He believes he is at the center of life and can affect what happens—he believes that his own thought process can influence objects and events in the world outside himself.

Because of this, he is unable to understand why his pet dies, or why he can't have what he wants when he wants it, or why he gets sick. He becomes disturbed with unfamiliar bodily changes that accompany illness, and he often believes he caused the illness. Sometimes he feels he was bad or something is defective about him and that's why something bad happened to him. He does not perceive life as unpredictable. We adults accept sudden events as part of life. In fact, Scripture teaches us that life is uncertain and we should expect problems and upsets to occur, but a child has difficulty grasping this.

Because young children are egocentric (centered on themselves), they fail to consider the viewpoints of others. This has nothing to do with being conceited; it is just a normal part of the developmental process. They take things for granted and do not realize that other people need clarification. It's not until a child reaches the age of about seven that he begins to distinguish between his perspective and someone else's.

Three- to six-year-olds talk past one another. They have their own private speech and may not be talking to anyone in particular. They are not concerned whether you understand their words or not. They just assume their words have more meaning than is there.

A young child takes things at face value — literally. When a parent says, "I'm sick and tired of the way you are acting," what does a child think? He catches the parent's anger, but he also believes the parent actually may be getting both "sick" and "tired."

Think of other phrases we say that can be misunderstood: "Keep your shirt on"; "Hold your horses"; "That's cool"; and so on. Try to enter the child's mind. If you could hear what he is thinking, you would be amazed!

A child puts two and two together and does not necessarily come up with four. His unique connections make sense to him but to no one else. A child may see illness and going to the football game as related because his father became seriously ill the last time he went to a football game. A child may even become anxious and avoid going to a game because of the connection he made.

When Brad was about six, he injured himself on the jungle gym at school, but he refused to tell his mother what had happened to him. After several days of questioning, all she could get him to say was, "I can't tell you." Over and over he would repeat this, sometimes even in tears. His mother was becoming increasingly alarmed over what really had happened to him until she began to make a connection. A friend of hers had died in a hospital just recently. Her son, she discovered, was afraid that if he told her what had happened, he would have to go to a hospital, and—in his mind—if he did, he would die.

Middle Childhood

For children of all ages, stressors vary in their intensity. In the middle childhood years, different degrees of stress can be felt from such things as a poor grade on a test, the loss of a pet frog, rejection or ridicule by a friend, moving, or the separation or divorce of parents. And remember—children are more limited in their coping than adults. They don't have the repertoire of experiences to draw upon when faced with stressors and some of these things can be extremely difficult for a child to cope with.

Travel back in time with me and picture yourself as a seven-year-old child. You and your parents have just moved, and this is your first day at a new school in the middle of a semester. You didn't sleep well last night. Your stomach doesn't feel good, and you have to go to the bathroom a lot.

As you walk down the hall to your new classroom, you see other children looking at you. Some of them are giggling. You feel like turning around and running. You open the classroom door and thirty strange faces turn around and stare at you. Your heart rate increases and your stomach tightens up. The teacher makes you the focus of attention by telling the class that you are the new student, and then she proceeds to ask you your name. But the words just won't come out of your mouth! That is stress! Do you remember what it was like?

Children from seven to twelve have changed considerably in their thinking. They have advanced in their ability to think conceptually. They are now able to work out some problems in their heads instead of just by trial and error. They can see the viewpoints of other people, and they recognize the feelings of others as well. Even their world of fantasy has changed. They now fantasize about real people and events instead of engaging in so much make-believe. They can make sense of stress.

Children in the middle years are usually enjoyable and uncomplicated, calm and educable, but they still have a difficult time dealing with anything that resembles intense stress. They prefer to avoid the issue and often will change the subject when you attempt to draw them into a discussion of their problems. They try to avoid the pain and anxiety. This is why so many people who work with children of this age use games and play in the therapy process. Play allows children an outlet for what they are feeling and gives the counselor the information sought. Communication toys such as tape recorders, phones, drawing materials and puppets are very helpful.

However, even though these children have developed considerably in their thinking processes, they still tend to jump to conclusions without considering all the facts. Actually, children of this age group have a tendency to listen to contradictory information and not see the inconsistency. They often do not understand what they are hearing. Sometimes these children will not understand adults who are talking to them, and another real problem is that the adults often do not realize they are not being understood.

Teenagers

As for teenagers, have you ever tried to talk to one and in exasperation found yourself asking, "Are you deaf?" because you got no answer? Don't feel alone!

Parents of teenagers everywhere are realizing that teens live in their own world, a world inside themselves. They are self-centered, and they often withdraw from contact with others.

They regard themselves as unique and special, and they tend to live in a state of either agony or ecstasy! Their subjectivity level is high. They are self-critical, and they assume others are critical of them, too. They become super-sensitive and are subject to quick shame and dramatic embarrassment. Social pressures peak and self-doubt and feelings of inferiority intensify.

Unfortunately, a teen's self-worth is nearly always dependent upon one of the most unstable pillars in existence—peer acceptance. One unstable group is trying to gain stability from another unstable group.

In answer to the question, "What is a teenager?" Bettie Youngs gives a thorough description in her book, *Helping Your Teenager Deal With Stress.*

1. The teen is a person who is leaving childhood and working through the stages of adolescence.
2. When this person is frightened, he (or she) tends to regress to the security of being a child and may behave accordingly.
3. Rapid and intense physiological and psychological changes are occurring.
4. The teenager desperately yearns for inde-

pendence, but does not have enough experience to be independent.

5. Teenagers have a great desire to express personal needs and to be taken seriously.

6. They have not yet firmly established their own internal value system.

7. They are still dependent upon the family, financially and emotionally.

8. Lasting life decisions may be made during this time.

9. They are alert to catch discrepancies between adults' behavior and the rules and values those adults express.

10. Teens have the same intense emotional needs and feelings adults have but lack understanding as to the meaning of those feelings and don't know how to cope with them.

11. Teens have a strong need to be mentored by adults whose guidance will assist them in developing personal identity.

12. When parents are absent physically or emotionally, teens feel lonely and isolated. They need parents to be present—to listen, to offer guidance, to show love and attention, to allow them to face life experiences, and to encourage independence and healthy adult-child separation.

13. Adult nurturing is needed for the teen to construct his own self-identity and develop competency.

14. If effective coping skills are not learned, teens become especially vulnerable to stressful situations.

15. If a teen feels that the family situation does not provide sufficient nurturing, he will turn to his

peer group for support.[1]

Teens of today are facing a unique set of pressures. Think with me a moment, and compare today with the time you were a teen. For example, did you have to face the possibility of a radioactive nuclear cloud circling the earth because of an atomic accident? Probably not, but today it has become a reality because of an accident at a nuclear plant in Russia. Did you have to face the threat of gang violence with two or three killings a night, every night of the week? Probably not, but in some areas of Southern California this situation is commonplace, and it is spreading to other parts of the country as well. What about AIDS? Most of us had never heard of AIDS when we were adolescents. Some of today's teens have already experienced the trauma of a friend or a family member dying from this disease.

Our present generation of teens lives under the potential of being the last generation. Even though they may not talk about it, they think about it. Wars have always been a part of life but not like today. Teens hear the same things you do through the media: threats of war, terrorist kidnappings, bombings, pollution, and social security funds running out before we reach the age of retirement. They are being raised in a promiscuous, violent, noncommittal, non-Christian society. It is a very me-centered society, and if your teen is a Christian, this in itself can create additional stress. A Christian teen is a minority person.

Moral choices are being made at an earlier age — choices about drugs, sex, friends and drinking. And to top it off, we now face the issue of AIDS and the emphasis on "safe sex."

There is another reason today's teens are more prone to difficulty in handling stress than other generations. It is not only because the rapid changes bring new pressures, but also that this generation has been given so much more in material things than previous generations have. Thus it is difficult for them to delay rewards. Instant solutions are important, and they don't know how to handle discouragement and disillusionment. As a result, they experience stress more readily, and many of them gravitate toward drugs, alcohol or even suicide.

Not all teens experience intense turmoil, but they all have their ups and down. Adolescence is one of the most difficult transitions of life. At best, it's a roller-coaster experience.

The volatile, emotional, up-and-down world of the teenager can throw parents into a turmoil. Some teens emulate a turtle and withdraw into a hard, sullen shell; others erupt like a Hawaiian volcano.

Cycle of Stress

A sequence of stressful situations where one upsetting experience leads to another can create what we call a "cycle of stress." Let's look in on a typical day in a teen's life and see how this cycle of stress develops:

1. Jerry's best friend stands him up at the donut shop before school. He then sees him driving in with a girl Jerry himself has a crush on.

2. When Jerry gets to school, he is upset and can't remember the combination for his locker. This makes him late for class and he can't hand in his assignment on time. Now he's really upset—he skipped his favorite TV show last night just so he could complete that boring assignment.

3. His teacher refuses to let him go to the office to get help with his locker, and she will not accept the late assignment.

4. As he walks back to his seat, Jerry trips over another student's pile of books in the aisle and the student swears at him and calls him a clumsy "_____."

5. Jerry swears back and threatens to punch him out. The teacher hears him but did not hear what the other student said. Jerry is given a half-hour detention.

6. The detention causes him to miss band practice.

7. Since he missed practice, he will not be allowed to go with the band and play at the Friday evening game in a neighboring town. This really infuriates him because the time on the bus with his friends is as important to Jerry as the game.

8. Upon arriving home he slams the door, cracking a window, and he snaps at his mom — who is fairly stressed out herself — and Jerry proceeds to get a lecture and a week's restriction.

Notice how one problem leads to another, and with each one Jerry seems to have less control.

A sequence of events like this, creating a cycle of stress, can happen to anyone. However, we can help our children and teens learn to interrupt the sequence and break the cycle so they can handle the problems in a much healthier manner. In this book we will look at ways to do that.

¤¤¤ **2** ¤¤¤

SOURCES OF STRESS

W hat is stress? Stress is any life situation that chronically bothers, irritates or upsets you. It is any type of action that places conflicting or heavy demands upon your body. What do these demands do? They simply upset the body's equilibrium.

Our bodies come equipped with a highly sophisticated defense system that helps us cope with those events in life which threaten and challenge us. When any of us feels pressured or threatened, our body quickly mobilizes its defenses for fight or flight. In the case of stress, we are infused with an abundance of adrenalin which disrupts our normal functioning and creates a heightened sense of arousal.

We are like a rubber band that is being stretched. Usually, when the pressure is released, the rubber band returns to normal. When it is stretched too much, though, or kept in that position too long, the rubber begins to lose its elasticity, becomes brittle and develops cracks. Eventually it breaks. That is similar to what happens to us if there is too much stress in our lives.

What is stressful to one individual, however, may not be stressful to another. For some, stress is worry about future events that cannot be avoided, and then concern about the events after they have occurred. For others stress is simply the wear and tear of life. It has been called an "influential force."

Although some people think of it as tension and some as anxiety, not all stress is bad. We need a certain amount of pressure and stimulation. Stress can be good if it is short-lived. Good stress is called *"eu*stress," from the Latin word *eu,* meaning good. It is positive and helpful because it does not last, nor is it experienced continuously. The body's equilibrium soon goes back to normal. When the body does not return to normal rest and recovery, we have bad stress, or *"dis*tress."

Causes of Stress

The stress in a child or teen's life can be caused when anything happens that . . .
- annoys him
- threatens him
- excites him
- scares him
- worries him
- hurries him
- frustrates him
- angers him
- challenges him
- embarrasses him
- reduces or threatens his self-esteem

Most of the time, however, it is not a particular *event* that causes stress. What then causes the problem? Most situations which produce stress involve some sort of *conflict* between ourselves and the world outside us. For example, if a teen skips school to go to the beach (which fulfills a personal desire), he creates a new problem at school with his absence. If a teen becomes over-involved at school and then has little time and energy for household responsibilities, there are new demands placed upon his family. If he doesn't balance the demands from outside with those from inside himself, he will experience stress and pressure.

Where does most of our stress come from? Whether we are children, teens or adults, it comes from our own minds. The most damaging stress comes from threats that cannot be acted upon since they exist only in our imagination. Some children and some teens imagine the worst in a situation (and so do some parents). They worry, which creates more threat and imagined fears. Even when there *is* a definite threat to the body, the problem is in the mind. Situations that worry a child can be the most troublesome of all. On the other hand, a person who has learned to live according to "Let not your heart be troubled, neither let it be afraid" (John 14:27) will be able to handle the pressures of life, both real and imagined, much better.

What kind of things do you think would cause children to experience stress? Listed on the next page are twenty situations that produce stress in a child. Which do *you* think are the most stressful? Pretend you are a child and rank these in order from 1 to 20 with 1 being the most stressful and 20 being the least.

At the end of this chapter we'll look at how the *children* rated these stress producers.

CHILDREN AND STRESS

_____ Wetting pants in class

_____ Having an operation

_____ Giving a report in class

_____ Having a scary dream

_____ Being sent to the principal's office

_____ Going blind

_____ Moving to a new school

_____ Going to the dentist

_____ Being made fun of in class

_____ Acquiring a baby sibling

_____ Being suspected of lying

_____ Being held back a year in school

_____ Not getting 100 on a test

_____ Getting lost

_____ Receiving a bad report card

_____ Losing a game

_____ Hearing parents quarrel

_____ Being caught stealing

_____ Losing a parent

_____ Being picked last for a team[1]

Other Contributors to Stress

It is important to consider several other major contributors to stress: lack of proper rest and sleep, improper diet and the "hurry disease," for instance. Putting pressure on children to perform or to hurry wires their emotions and their bodies, and it makes relaxing difficult.

Let's consider now some of the sources of that stress. For example, can you remember what bothered you when you were in grade school? The fears, frustrations, uncertainties, pressures? Here, according to grade level, are some of the most common things that cause elementary schoolchildren to experience stress:

In *Kindergarten* the main stressors are uncertainty, fear of abandonment by an important adult, fear of wetting themselves, and fear of punishment or reprimand from their teacher.

First grade stressors are fear of riding the bus, fear of wetting in class, teacher disapproval, ridicule by peers, receiving the first report card, and fear of not passing to second grade.

In *second grade* the stressors include not understanding a certain lesson, fear of the teacher's discipline, fear of being different in some way from other children in the class, and, often, missing a particular parent.

In *third grade* stress is felt from fear of being chosen last on any team or for any activity, having to stay after school, a parent-teacher conference, fear of peer disapproval, fear of not being liked by the teacher, fear of test taking, and not enough time to finish a test or assignment.

In *fourth grade* the stressors are fear of being chosen last for anything, fear of peer disapproval of dress or appearance, fear that their friends will find new friends and share their "secrets," fear of peer ridicule, and fear of not being liked by the teacher.

In *fifth grade* the stressors are just about the same as in fourth, but there is another concern as well, that of the possibility of not being promoted and thus not being a "big sixth-grader" the next year.

In *sixth grade* there are some lingering and some

new stressors such as the fear of being chosen last for anything, peer disapproval of appearance, feeling unpopular, fear of the unknown concerning developing sexuality, and fear of not passing to junior high — as well as fear of *going* to junior high.

These are just the stressors of school. When you add to this list all the things connected to the other parts of a child's life, you discover a multitude of potential stressors,[2] and you realize that the potential for stress is all around us.

Think about the world of our children and our teens for a moment. All day they experience stimuli which can produce stress. The very state of change and flux they are in creates stress for them. Whether stress becomes a problem for them depends on how much of it they experience and how long it lasts.

To top all that off, our kids experience most of what we adults experience as well: time pressure, high expectations, divorce in the family, illness, failure, violence, jealousy, etc.

Have you ever asked your teen what he worries about regarding the future? You might want to share some of the worries you remember having when you were a teen as a way of encouraging him to open up and share with you.

The Three Stress Situations of Life

To become aware of stress in a teen's life so as to be prepared to help him, the best way to start is by identifying the three major categories of stress.

Type A Stress

The first is called *Type A* (not to be confused with the "Type A Personality") and is both *foreseeable and avoidable.* If a teen plans to ride "The Killer" roller-coaster ride or see one of the newest blood-and-gore science-fiction movies, he knows in advance the stress he will encounter and is able to avoid it if he so desires.

There is also foreseeable and avoidable stress which is not under the teen's control. The world lives under the threat of running out of natural resources and seeing the environment become more and more polluted. Another threat is the ever-present possibility of nuclear war. Stress from these types of uncertainties is difficult for anyone to handle.

Type B Stress

Type B stress situations come from demands which are *neither foreseeable nor avoidable.* These fall into the category of crisis events such as the death of a friend or family member, an accident while in the car or while involved in sports activities, the discovery of his parents' impending divorce or separation, or learning that a sibling is gay or has AIDS.

These stressful situations place the greatest demands upon teens.

They must handle their own feelings, the situation itself, and the responses of other people as well. Both the adolescent who has to face the divorce of his parents and the teen with a torn tendon which eliminates his chances of a college sports scholarship have to adjust in two main ways: (1) thinking about themselves with a new perspective; and (2) relating to others in a different fashion.

Type C Stress

The third type of stress situation, *Type C,* is *foreseeable but not avoidable.* What kinds of situations are

foreseeable but unavoidable? Facing parents after vio-
lating curfew. Exams. Taking a three-week trip in the
car with a family of five. Being drafted into the military
during wartime.

Major Stresses/Problems

We know there are countless sources of stress for
teens today. In 1986 an extensive survey was conducted
by *Children and Teens Today*. The readership of this
magazine has a common element—whether they are
ministers, lay counselors, therapists, administrators or
counselors, they all work directly with children and/or
adolescents.

The question was: What do you see as the major
stresses/problems facing today's teenagers? Of eight
suggested answers given, 72.4 percent of those who
responded listed "problems arising from parental
divorce/remarriage," with "peer pressure to drink/al-
coholism" coming in second at 68.2 percent. Here is how
people pinpointed the remaining six problems listed:

59%–acceptance of sexual intercourse/experimen-
   tation at a young age;

48%–pressure to experiment with drugs;

45%–depression;

30%–the need to attain academic excellence;

28%–attempts at suicide;

23%–fears arising from the threat of nuclear war.

The readers were invited to describe other major
problems which were not listed, and the problems mentioned most often were parent and family-related difficulties.[3]

Let's look at an adult stress study and apply it to
the lives of children and teens. The Holmes-Rahe Life

Event Scale[4] serves as our example.

You will find below the forty-three life events listed in that scale. They have been adjusted to fit situations in the life of a child — that is, "spouse" is changed to "parent," "work" to "school," etc. The point value of each life event remains the same.

LIFE EVENTS

1. Death of a parent 100
2. Divorce of parents 73
3. Separation of parents 65
4. Parent's jail term 63
5. Death of a close family member (e.g., a grandparent) 63
6. Personal injury or illness 53
7. Parent's remarriage 50
8. Suspension or expulsion from school 47
9. Parents' reconciliation 45
10. Long vacation (Christmas, summer, etc.) . . . 45
11. Parent's or sibling's sickness 44
12. Mother's pregnancy 40
13. Anxiety over sex 39
14. Birth of new baby (or adoption) 39
15. New school, classroom or teacher 39
16. Money problems at home 38
17. Death (or moving away) of close friend 37
18. Change in studies 36
19. More quarrels with parents 36
20. (Not applicable to a child or teen)
21. (Not applicable to a child or teen)

Totaling the score, you may be surprised to find how quickly an average child can reach the 300-point level of severe stress potential. Changes occur rapidly in a child's life, far more rapidly than in the life of his parents. Six hours of school alone can subject him to the possibility of any combination of life events 8, 10, 15, 18, 22, 25, 27, 31 or 43 on almost a routine basis. In addition, the ups and downs of his social life add the chance of stress from life events 13, 17, 32, 36, 39, or 41. He is especially susceptible to personal injury because of the high percentage of his time spent in physical activities such as bike riding or skating. In addition, he may fall victim to any contagious disease that strikes the school.

We as parents cannot eliminate all the stresses of a child's life. Some of them will always be there, but we can do the following:

1. Realize that our children live under constant stress.
2. Recognize any stressors that we or our environment tend to place on a child.
3. Take steps to eliminate those stressors which can be eliminated.
4. Teach our children how to handle the stressors of life.[5]

On the next page are the stress-producing situations listed on page 22 in the order in which the children perceived them, from most stressful to least stressful.

KIDS' RESPONSES TO CHILDREN AND STRESS

1. Losing a parent
2. Going blind
3. Being held back a year in school
4. Wetting pants in school
5. Hearing parents quarrel
6. Being caught stealing
7. Being suspected of lying
8. Receiving a bad report card
9. Being sent to the principal's office
10. Having an operation
11. Getting lost
12. Being made fun of in class
13. Moving to a new school
14. Having a scary dream
15. Not getting 100 on a test
16. Being picked last for a team
17. Losing in a game
18. Going to the dentist
19. Giving a report in class
20. Acquiring a baby sibling[6]

Compare your answers with those of the children here. How close did you come? If you are like most parents, you will be surprised by the results. Does this make you want to listen more closely to your children?

Why not ask your own children to rank these in the same way for themselves? You may be surprised.

¤¤¤ **3** ¤¤¤

SYMPTOMS
OF STRESS

Each and every day we face the possibility of stress. As adults we just
accept that we will encounter pressure and tension in our lives. However,
we sometimes fail to realize that a child
can be stressed every bit as much or even
more than we are. After all, we have lived
longer and have developed some coping skills. A young
child is still in the formative stages of his or her life. He
doesn't have the coping ability that we do, and when a
child is stressed, he will show it in one way or another.

Symptoms of Stress in Your Young Child

You may be asking, "How do I know if my child
is under a lot of stress?"

There are many symptoms. If these symptoms
occur frequently and persistently, listen to the message
that's being given to you.

31

Some of the symptoms are:

— chronic irritability
— difficulty concentrating
— difficulty sleeping or difficulty staying awake
— poor eating habits such as impulsive, uncontrolled eating
— restlessness
— rapid heart rate
— backaches
— neckaches
— headaches
— muscles aching for no apparent reason
— irritating behavior
— lack of spontaneity
— frequent mood shifts
— nervous habits such as twitches, nail biting, pulling at hair, biting lips

If you notice these signs, especially a combination of them, you can be fairly sure your child needs help to learn to respond to life in a healthier manner

Teaching Your Child to Spot Stress

Childhood is a long time of life, a time of preparation, growth and development. During this period, children face some of the same stressors as adults, but without the same resources. You can help your child by explaining what stress is and teaching him how to recognize it when it occurs. You can help him monitor his own life. This can be done best by helping the child recognize the symptoms of stress.

If your child came to you and asked, "What is stress? How do I know when I have it?" what would you say? How would you describe stress to a child?

Perhaps you could say, "Stress can result from what happens between people. Your friend may be mad at you, or the students in class may have made fun of you and it really hurt. It can occur when you don't get enough sleep or when there is too much going on. In addition, you can cause your own stress by what you think about yourself. If you think you're dumb or no good or not pretty, those ideas can cause stress."

In explaining what stress is to your child, you may want to use this "Have you ever . . . ?" approach:

Have you ever had your heart beat faster?
Have you ever had your hands get cold and sweaty?
Have you ever had your stomach get in a knot?
Have you ever had your tummy hurt?
Have you ever gotten nervous?
Have you ever felt sad or giggled a lot?
Have you ever felt mean, or like crying, or that you wanted to get back at someone?
Have you ever had frightening dreams?
Have you ever not been able to concentrate?
Have you ever been grouchy?
Have you ever not gotten along with other people?
(And any other questions you can think of.)

If a child understands that these symptoms could be caused by stress, it can help him monitor his own life and be able to put to use some of the stress reduction suggestions given later in this book.

Spotting Stress in Your Teen

Teens face stressful situations continually. If a peer group uses drugs or alcohol, for example, or engages in petty theft, the people in the group will pressure your teen to participate. Yet he knows that the consequences will create additional pressure through the response of parents, church leaders and teachers, and according to his own value system.

The one issue which affects a teen's response to stress more often than all others is the development of his own identity.

Instability of emotional expression is a normal characteristic of this turbulent quest, and the state of an adolescent's identity fluctuates continually.

The teen's identity starts to develop as he begins to withdraw from his parents. He becomes a "separate" person by rejecting customary family patterns.

This is the time he begins to determine what is important to him, establish his own value system, and develop his own unique personality and identity.

A teen doesn't have to have a certain type of personality in order to have a solid identity. Some are outgoing and some are introverted. Some are factually oriented and some are quite emotional in their response to life.

In order to recognize when your teen shows signs of reacting to stress, it will help if you understand the two basic types of teenage identities, the *integrated* and the *non-integrated*. The integrated identity is one in which attitudes, values and abilities are connected with one another in a harmonious manner. The non-integrated identity is built upon a set of attitudes, values and habits which are more or less unconnected and could be in conflict. Teens with non-integrated identities often feel they have to choose between looking out for themselves and giving in to others. They mismanage stress because their inner conflicts create inner stress and make it difficult for them to respond in a positive manner to the outward situations.

Reactions to Type A Situations

In a Type A stress situation, the non-integrated teen will usually be either an anxious teen or a conforming teen. The anxious teen, when confronted with a foreseeable but avoidable problem, will worry and stew over his decision. He has difficulty deciding whether to give in or try to avoid the situation. He may instead come up with an alternative: He may get sick. Headaches, psychosomatic symptoms, fatigue, boredom and stomach aches are common. Because of low self-esteem and a disconnected set of values and attitudes, this teen tends to avoid the stressful situation in a self-punishing manner.

With the other non-integrated response, which is to conform, the teen is looking for a "quick-fix" to alleviate the stress while at the same time gaining peer group approval and acceptance. Remember, the peer group's influence is the most powerful on the teen who has this non-integrated identity. He lacks the inner strength to resist conforming. He wants to grow up and become independent, but does not know how. However, conforming brings about its own set of problems and stresses which the teen does not think about and which continue to compound the problem.

Reactions to Type B Situations

Type B situations, those which are both unforeseeable and unavoidable, are difficult not only for teens, but for adults as well. They are often very intense, and they tend to disrupt our life plans. For teens, these can be devastating since they undermine an already fragile sense of self-esteem.

People react in a number of different ways when hit by a crisis. Integrated teens, those who cope well in a Type B crisis situation, are those who:

- have another person who stands by them and gives support;
- understand the meaning of what they have lost in the crisis;
- are able to handle their own feelings of guilt;
- have a reason to live — they have hope;
- have a biblical perspective on life (these teens respond the best).

(For additional information, see the chapter entitled "The Questions of Life" in *How to Have a Creative Crisis* by this author.[1])

It is actually possible to predict which teens will have the most difficulty in a Type B situation. Those with a non-integrated personality can be overwhelmed in a crisis because they are emotionally weak. They often respond in ways that make the problem worse.

If they are physically ailing, they do not have the best resources with which to respond.

If they deny the problem or tend to deny reality most of the time, they struggle with understanding and acceptance.

If they have the tendency to talk, eat or drink excessively, they tend to exaggerate those behaviors and make matters worse.

If they are impulsive and have to have problems fixed "immediately," or if they tend to procrastinate, the problem becomes greater.

Blamers have a hard time coping with a crisis. They ask, "Who caused the problem?" rather than asking, "What's the solution?"

Those who are overly dependent cling to others and those who are independent avoid any assistance. Each of these reactions feeds the problem.

Type B situations are viewed not as events which could happen to any teen but as difficulties specifically directed toward them, either because of bad luck or because that's the way life is! Some teens feel they are the only ones to have these problems, and they tend to become self-punishers. They behave in a manner that pushes others away, and they tend not to trust anyone—other teens or adults.

Another response is that of competition and challenge. Some teens feel they can change their luck so they challenge the problem without adequate planning or anticipation of the consequences. They could become addicted to the challenge, and they could even cheat or steal in order to resolve the problem.

Reactions to Type C Stress Situations

In the Type C stress situation, which is foreseeable but not avoidable, a common reaction is anger. Going to the dentist, taking an exam, or having to take a vacation with abusive parents—each falls into the Type C category. It could include doing chores or homework. Many teens have difficulty with these situations and often make it miserable for others around them.

Each situation becomes a war zone over power

and control. Everything involves a struggle and the teen usually has an excuse. He projects blame onto other people or events. If you're the parent of such a teen, don't be surprised if you feel a great deal of anger yourself. These teens have the ability to provoke this response. Their display of cool control and arrogance is a cover-up for their inner feelings of fragmentation.

Other teens, however, respond with a great deal of fear. Some develop phobias about school. Teens who live in homes where there is physical abuse, substance abuse, or continual rejection are often fearful. A frightened teen looks to others for solutions to his problems and often will do almost anything if someone accepts him and is kind to him.

Teens' Coping Techniques

A common coping technique is to run away from home. It is estimated that approximately one million teens run away each year. These teens are open to exploitation. They don't blame others, though; they blame themselves.

Often a teen responds with behavior that has a hidden message. For example, self-mutilating teens, through their deliberate and radical behavior, express their independence. This behavior also can be their way of trying to control their fears, sexual thoughts, or violent and aggressive impulses. In talking to a teen, you may hear him say, "It's my body and I will do with it what I want, and nobody can stop me. Just try. It won't work." Any efforts to control their outward behavior without dealing with their inner feelings will be ineffective.

Alienation and personality restriction is another means of expressing depression and stress. Many older teens feel apathetic and out of touch with themselves and others, which results in inaction. The teen avoids anything that might lead to a failure and any aspiration that could bring disappointment. He will not expose himself to any heartache. He is not a risk taker.

Sometimes a teen will unwittingly adopt a particular role in order to handle the stresses in his life. Let's consider some of these roles in light of what the teen is trying to accomplish.

Some teens are *dreamers.* This often happens when they are bored. They dream about how life could be better, or they begin to imagine a new type of life. Do you know what your teen's daydreams are? Have you ever shared some of your own that you had when you were a teen, or even now? Talking about your own dreams may open the door for you to discover your teen's fantasies as well.

Some teens are *complainers.* They collect grievances, and they gripe and complain about friends, teachers, parents, school, and anything that walks in front of them. Making something or someone else look bad makes them feel better. They lessen their stress feelings by blaming others.

Other teens are *brooders.* They say very little outwardly, but a great deal goes on inside their minds. They often focus on how unfair life is.

The *joker* reacts in the opposite way. He doesn't seem to take life seriously at all. This is often a mask hiding the teen's insecurity and fear of getting close to others. The humor is used to avoid intimacy and also to gain attention and recognition.

Some teens are *charmers.* They know how to manipulate others and often act years younger than they are. It seems to work for them. Though they are charming, they appear to be somewhat incapable and dependent. This is their way of coping.

Have you ever come across the *excuse maker?* If he's late, it's someone else's fault. To handle stress, he gives an excuse. He avoids the pain of personal responsibility. This is his way of lessening his own stress.

Other teens become *escape artists* in an effort to avoid their problems. They escape into school activities, their church, hobbies, sports, etc., but they never get around to resolving the situation that is creating the stress.

Some become *actors* to handle their stress. They deny their pain or loss or that they are upset, and they seem to get on with their lives. Unfortunately, we often tend to encourage their denials by saying, "How well you are handling that upsetting situation!"

These non-integrated teens need a lot of help. Often they will need more help than we as parents can provide. The help could include support groups, counseling or even family therapy. Without help, these teens will get worse before they get better—and getting better does not usually happen naturally.

The non-integrated teen is unable to avoid, cope with, or prepare for stress. To make matters worse, he tends to create and expose himself to more stress—which turns into a vicious cycle. Because of the additional stress he experiences and creates, he has to spend more time and emotional energy trying to cope, and that leaves less of those two vital elements for healthy growth. Each of his teen years, then, brings additional stress, which he is less and less capable of handling.[2]

Stress Overload

What are the major symptoms of stress overload? There are a number of signals that make this easy to detect. Which of these symptoms are evident in your teen?

_____ Difficulties in making both major and minor decisions.

_____ Excessive daydreaming or fantasizing about "getting away from it all."

_____ Increased use of cigarettes, alcohol, stimulants or tranquilizers.

_____ Thoughts trailing off while speaking or writing. The person wonders, *What am I saying?* and can't understand why he loses his train of thought.

_____ Excessive worrying about all areas of life; taking on almost everyone else's worries in addition to his own.

_____ Sudden outbursts of temper and hostility.

_____ Paranoid ideas and mistrust of friends and family.

_____ Forgetfulness of appointments, deadlines and dates.

_____ Frequent spells of brooding and feelings of inadequacy.

_____ Reversals in usual behavior. People say, "He acts like a different person."[3]

Recognizing the symptoms is a big step toward identifying the problems and can point you in the right direction to find and implement possible solutions.

On the other hand, some teens are able to face their problems themselves. They have the ability to confront their difficulties and to find ways to resolve them. Many teens are able to do this because of the inner faith they have in Jesus Christ and because they have learned to rely on God. They have discovered that their strength and stability come from being dependent on Him.

¤¤¤ 4 ¤¤¤

IDENTIFYING THE PROBLEMS

A s we noted in the last chapter, one of the biggest sources of upset for a child, especially a teen, is the development of his identity. Yet everyone has to go through it in order to reach adulthood. Dr. Keith Olson says it is necessary for a person to "develop a sense of personal identity that consistently establishes who he is as an integrated individual throughout each life role, separate and different from every other person."[1]

If a child has a healthy identity and a good sense of self-esteem, he will be better able to evaluate the risk of not giving in to outside pressures. The momentary satisfaction of peer group approval is not nearly as important as his lasting sense of self-respect. A person must learn to say no to his peers and handle the pressure he receives from them in return. Our goal as parents and teachers is to help our children and our teens develop a strong sense of positive identity and help them anticipate the pressures that will be exerted by their peer group and know how to respond to them.

As a child reaches his teen years, he begins to venture out from the family shores, but in such a way that he does not completely sever his family ties and support. This is a bit like walking a tightrope for the parents. Their main task at this time is to start relinquishing control, bit by bit, the right amount at the right time, as the teen spends more time with his peers and less with his parents. A balance of freedom and parental control is necessary if the teen is to learn through experience how to handle stress.

Eventually a teen pushes off completely from the safe shoreline of his parents and paddles for several years through turbulent waters of maturing until he reaches the theoretically "calmer" shores of adulthood. Teens experience many crises during these transitional years, and their efforts to find and be themselves sometimes give rise to intense frustrations.

Why do some teenagers seem to handle the transition of adolescence so well while others seem to be stress-prone, going straight from one stressful situation to another? Can we in some way identify these stress-prone individuals? Yes, there is a way. Everyone has the potential to be overwhelmed by stress, but some have greater difficulty than others with the pressures of life.

One type of stress-prone teen, or younger child, is very obvious. Perhaps you know one like this. He (or she) is always in a hurry, has to be the best, tends to take on too much for himself, often interrupts or over-reacts to others, and has difficulty losing. The number of students who manifest these characteristics seems to be greater in suburban schools than in rural ones. That could be because of the intense competitiveness among those whose upper-middle-class parents have chosen to make their homes in the suburbs.

These pressured kids tend to compete excessively for grades. I've even seen some who are not satisfied unless they receive the top *A* in the class. They are over-ambitious and have great difficulty handling disappointments. You won't find them having an easy time relaxing. They over-involve themselves in whatever they do, and when a goal is attained, they quickly search for another. Participation in and of itself is not sufficient. They must also achieve recognition.

These children and young people are well on the way to becoming classic Type A adults. This tendency doesn't usually begin in adulthood—it begins in childhood and becomes more evident during the teen years. This type of personality carries with it the possibility of a premature heart attack.

Another way to identify the person who has difficulty with stress but whose symptoms are not quite so obvious is by using an adaptation of the "Capable Kid Test" below. This test originally was designed for children but I feel it can be applied to teens as well. Identifying a child or teen's attitude and noting his comments regarding stressful situations will tell you much about his state.

THE CAPABLE KID TEST

Step 1. Think of a situation that your child or teen has experienced as stressful. It could be sharing a room or the car with a sibling, having a favorite weekend or a date cancelled, flunking a test, not making the school team or play, being shunned by friends, being embarrassed, etc.

Step 2. Think about how he reacted and whether that is his typical response to that type of situation.

Step 3. Choose **one** statement from the following list that best describes his reactions. (Select the first one that strikes you as appropriate.)

1. "Things like this always happen to me."
2. He becomes unreasonably quiet and walks away.
3. "I never get what I want. Nobody cares about me." (May become belligerent and verbally abusive.)
4. "Boy, am I disappointed." Then a few seconds later, "Oh, well, maybe it will work out the next time."
5. "This is no surprise. I was expecting something cruddy like this to happen." (Then becomes withdrawn and preoccupied.)
6. "That sure makes me angry, but I didn't know. Is there anything I can do about it now?"
7. "That is not fair. It's just not fair!" (And proceeds to have a child's or adolescent's temper tantrum.)
8. Doesn't visibly react, but just withdraws. He won't talk about it and tends to isolate himself.

Step 4. Now, find the description of your child or teen as indicated below. (Remember, the description you select should be his typical way of responding.) This will clarify for you the level of ability your child or teen has to handle stress.

#4 or #6—Either of these responses indicate a capable person. He handles stress well. This person will express his disappointment or anger and then quickly figure out what to do about it. He will be disappointed rather than greatly upset, and it will last for only a few minutes.

#1, #2 or #7—This is a slightly vulnerable child or teen. He has upset reactions, but they don't last long. He soon calms down, becomes less preoccupied with himself, and begins to make statements about how he can handle the problem. He could learn some new ways of coping so he wouldn't be so reactive.

#3, #5 or #8—This person is seriously vulnerable. His response usually lasts more than twenty-four hours, and symptoms of being vulnerable are evident in his life.[2]

Here are some of the most important characteristics of the capable child (or teen) and the vulnerable one:

The Capable Child

- resourceful
- confident
- able to confront people or situations when concerned or upset about something
- willing to take risks
- relaxed
- responsible
- able to express feelings easily
- endowed with a sense of direction

The Vulnerable Child

- withdrawn, preoccupied
- often sick without an organic cause
- isolated
- secretive, noncommunicative
- belligerent, uncooperative
- overly sensitive
- in need of excessive reassurance

**Identifying Sources of Stress
in Your Child or Teen**

Whenever you observe the symptoms of stress in your child, you need to identify the source. Look for its beginnings. You may want to ask yourself some of the following questions:

- Where is the source of this stress? Is it within the family (such as Dad taking a new job which requires frequent absences)? Or is it outside the family (perhaps failing a major math test)?

- Does the stress affect all the family members (as with a death), or just the child (having a close friend move away) or teen (a breakup with a romantic interest)?

- Was this stressful experience sudden (an accident or illness) or did it come on gradually (observing a close friend get sick and then die or watching a close friend become addicted)?

- What is the degree of the stress? Is it intense (a death of someone close) or mild (a cold which causes the child to miss a ball game)?

- Does this stressor require a short-term adjustment (arguing with a friend) or is it long-term (mononucleosis)?

- Was the situation expected (knowing a close friend is moving) or was it unexpected and unpredictable (a fire in the home)?

- Do the family members feel the stressor is one which can be adjusted to fairly soon (going to a new school) or is it beyond anyone's control (terminally ill parent with no prospects in sight for improvement)?

You will be enabled to help your child on a more long-term basis as you continue to be aware of every stressful situation. Each one carries with it both pain and potential for growth.

Identifying Stressors Peculiar to Teens

What creates stress for teens? If you can identify the sources of stress in your teen's life, you can help him learn to handle some of his stress-potential situations, and he will be better equipped then to handle other crises he may face as he approaches maturity.

Several factors that can bring about stress apply particularly to teens. I encourage you to look for any of these conditions in your teen's life:

1. *Boredom or lack of meaning.* That this leads to stress may sound strange, yet many teens do not find a challenge or meaning for their existence. This is an opportunity for you to help your teen discover the meaning that Christ gives to life. Helping a teen see life through God's perspective can bring meaning no matter what the teen is doing or what is happening to him.

2. *Time pressures and deadlines.* The stress these create is often of our own doing. Some children today are growing up hurried, and this continues into adulthood. What they see on television, in movies and from advertisers hurries them along the road toward being "grown up" before they can handle it emotionally.

3. *An excessive workload.* The pressure this creates is many times self-induced. Many teens will take on too many activities and be involved in too many things at one time.

4. *Unrealistic expectations* of oneself or of another person (e.g., teacher or parent). This can lead to

dissatisfaction. Suggest to your teen that he do the following:

a. List the expectations he thinks his parents have of him.

b. Itemize each of his expectations of himself.

c. Identify where each came from.

d. Think about and answer this question: "Why are these expectations important and how would my life be affected if they were not met?"

5. *Role conflicts.* Teens may be involved in activities or classes that do not fit their gifts, capabilities or interests, and they may feel stuck—and this creates tension.

6. *School environment.* A monotonous and repetitious environment can be just as much a problem as a fast-paced, pressure-filled, competitive atmosphere. School can be very stressful. Having six to eight classes a day with different teachers and a different set of peers in each class can be disruptive. Having a report due, or a test scheduled, the same week in each class can be stressful. If the curriculum is too demanding or too boring and unchallenging for the teen's level of ability, this too can be stressful. If the teen does not understand an assignment and there is little help available from the teacher, the pressure and frustration can build.

7. *Lack of communication in a relationship.* When open communication and an open show of emotions are blocked, it is not only stressful but also discouraging and can lead to depression in the life of a person who already has low self-esteem. If a teen has uncertainties about his relationship with a friend or with his parents, stress could be

present.

8. *A performance-based self-esteem.* Those who build their sense of identity and self-esteem upon an inadequate basis such as work, appearance, grades or athletic ability will experience a great deal of pressure and tension.

9. *The Type A personality.* This becomes a major cause of stress for the teen himself as well as for other family members and for fellow workers. The tendency starts in childhood and many teens are prone to be overly influenced by this "hurry-up" pressure.

10. *Loud and excessively rhythmic music.* What does music mean to a teen? It may be an expression of uniqueness, rebellion or peer group involvement. For some teens it is a way to assert independence and power.[3] Neither teens nor adults, however, realize how much stress is produced by the "noise" many teens call music. Unfortunately, many parents take the attitude, "Oh, well, that's just a phase he's going through. It's loud and unintelligible, but I guess it's not all that bad."

Isn't it? Let's consider the effect of music.

Some music can stimulate romantic feelings; other music can create a feeling of sadness or depression. Some music peps us up and makes us move faster. Researchers have proven that our bodies respond to sounds whether the sound registers consciously or unconsciously.

Radionics is the study of the effect of vibrations on the health and strength of the body. It focuses especially on how muscles and organs respond to sound.

Did you know that musical rhythms physically affect your teen's brain and heart? Did you know that both hard and soft rock create physiological and psychological tension and can disrupt the inner rhythm of the body? And that disco music, with its mix of instruments and volume, produces stress on the body? Insistent rhythms can arouse agitated feelings which include tension, excitement and even sexual arousal.

Too much sound can lead to annoyance, frustration and distraction—stress that can lower the quality of a person's emotional life. According to former Surgeon General of the United States Dr. William H. Stewart, too much continual noise can create adverse physiological changes in the body's cardiovascular, glandular and respiratory system. It can also cause stress on the muscular responses.

You have the right, for your own sanity's sake and to maintain control of your own stress level as well as to help your teen, to exercise control over the volume of the music, what is played, and when it is played.

Effects of Stress on Others

You should be aware of the fact that others in the family are always affected when any member experiences stress. Stress does not usually become evident in just one person. The situation which causes the stress for that person nearly always causes stress, although at various levels, for others in the home as well.

The following activity will help you evaluate stress levels among the various members of your family. Let me suggest that you ask each person to complete this evaluation, and then share your responses with one another.

STRESS EVALUATION

1. When have you experienced the greatest amount of stress during the last five years? What contributed to this stress?

Time	Cause	Who did you share this with?
Present to 1 year ago		
1-2 years ago		
2-3 years ago		
3-4 years ago		
4-5 years ago		

2. During the last five years, which family member do you think has experienced the greatest amount of stress, and what contributed to that stress?

Time	Cause	Who did the person share this with?
Present to 1 year ago		
1-2 years ago		
2-3 years ago		
3-4 years ago		
4-5 years ago		

3. Indicate which, if any, of these possible circumstances or conditions could cause stress for you:

_____ Boredom or lack of memory

_____ Time pressures and deadlines

_____ Excessive workload

_____ Unrealistic expectations

_____ Perfectionism

_____ Role conflicts

_____ Blocked emotions

_____ Environment

_____ Concern over a relationship

_____ Inflexibility

_____ Identity and self-esteem built upon an inadequate basis

_____ Type A personality tendencies

_____ Music and noise

As stress in the entire family is identified, dealt with and reduced, the stressed teen will benefit in several ways—through direct changes in his own life as well as through adjustments in his environment. Healthier and happier family relationships can be a transformation welcomed by everyone in the home.

5

FEARS

One way to understand the stressors of children is to understand their fears. Why? Because so much childhood stress stems from fear.

How do we recognize a child's fears? What indicates that anxiety is present?

Some children are quite verbal about their fears and you have little difficulty being aware. Others either avoid thinking about them or make it a point not to share them. However, whether he talks about it openly or not, if a child is fearful or troubled with anxiety, you probably will notice some of the following symptoms.

Symptoms of Fear

Children who have difficulty concentrating and who become either listless or hyperactive may be struggling with inner anxiety. They could be experiencing stress. If their appetite changes from eating very little to consuming greater amounts of food, this too could be a sign of anxiety. Bedwetting, nightmares, restlessness, insomnia, unusual talkativeness, stuttering, panic attacks, compulsive behaviors or obsessive thought patterns are additional indications of fear. Often a wide range of bodily complaints will be the indication of fear, or it may accompany any of the above.

One grandmother said to me, "I can always tell how my daughter and son-in-law are getting along by how much my granddaughter is stuttering."

Some Specific Basic Fears

Let's look at some of the basic fears of childhood as suggested by Erik Erikson (who has pioneered studies in the developmental stages of life).

Children fear **withdrawal of support**. This pressure can be felt both at home and at school, and children fear the withdrawal of peers as well as that of adults. Being too smart or not smart enough can turn peers away. Wearing the wrong clothes can have the same effect!

QUESTIONS (to ask your child): What kind of help do you like? How do you feel when someone takes it away? How can you handle this?

Children fear **suddenness**. Infants respond to sudden movements around them with a startled response. This continues throughout childhood. Adults may plan deliberately for some time to make major moves such as taking a new job and moving into a new home in another state, but for the child, it doesn't become a reality until it happens. This is true even if it has been discussed with him before. He needs much talk and anticipatory planning.

QUESTIONS: What kind of sudden, unexpected things frighten you most? How can we learn to handle these?

Fear of **noise** takes its toll on children, even infants, and we live in a noisy world. Four-month-old Lee became visibly agitated when his mother set a wound-up music box down beside him and turned it on. She had to take it away.

QUESTIONS: What noises bother you the most? How can you learn to handle noise?

Fear of **interruption** can be a real frustration to a child. A child's concentration on an activity can be intense, but an adult often will interrupt since, from the adult's perspective, that activity isn't important. However, playing, reading, talking, watching TV, or even just sitting around — any of these can be extremely meaningful activities for a child.

QUESTIONS: What interruptions bother you most? How can you handle those that can't be avoided?

Children fear **having something important to them taken away**. If you are a parent, you already know how possessive children feel about "their" things. These can be tangible things such as a rock collection, or they can be something intangible such as being the best student in the class. The child fears losing either.

QUESTIONS: What are you most afraid of losing? How can you handle losing something?

You know that children are afraid of too much restraint, but do you know they also fear **too much freedom**? Children do not like to be tied down to too many rules or restrictions, but an overabundance of freedom gives them more independence than they can handle. A balance is needed between parents and schools being restrictive and permissive.

QUESTIONS: What kinds of restrictions or rules bother you the most? What are the times you wish there were more rules or restrictions? What can you do when there are too many or not enough rules? How can you learn to handle this?

Children fear **being exposed**. In school, one question many children dread hearing is the one that comes when a test paper has been returned and the child has seen his bad grade—his friend turns around and asks, "What did you get?" Children feel exposed when they try for the honor roll and don't make it. Some children experience exposure when their parents listen in on their private conversations on the phone—these children learn to be secretive.

QUESTIONS: How do you feel when someone finds out something about you that you don't want them to know? What could you say or do to handle that better?

Strange as it seems, many children fear **being small** or remaining small. One of the status symbols in our society is bigness. Big houses, big athletes, big babies—all are given notice. In school, older students appear so large to a child that his own shortness is magnified. Boys are concerned about the size of their penis and girls want to be the first in their group to wear a bra. What does a child feel when others call him or her "Shorty"?

QUESTIONS: How do you feel about your size? What size do you want to become? What will you do if you end up smaller than that?

A fear common to both adults and children is

being left alone. Girls, especially, feel this fear, which accounts for the strong cliques preteen girls form.

Separation from mother is one of a child's greatest fears. Unfortunately, we live in a society where children are separated from their parents a great deal — because of divorce, both parents working, too many outside activities, pressures at home, or neglect. In school, children are upset when a favorite teacher leaves or when they are punished by being isolated from the rest of the class.

QUESTIONS: How do you feel when you are left alone? When might you be afraid of being alone? What does it feel like to be lonely? What can you do to handle the lonely times?

More Fears

In addition to those listed above, here are two more common childhood fears, along with some suggestions as to what can be done about them.

For many children an **animal** is an object of fear. (It is for many adults as well.) How do you help a child who is afraid of an animal? One thing you *don't* do is force the child to face the fear all at once, for he does not have the resources to cope with it.

Let's assume that a child is afraid of cats. A cat may appear small to us, but look at it from the child's point of view. A thirty-pound child looking at a ten- or fifteen-pound cat sees something very different from what you and I see. If you can imagine a cat that is half or a third of your weight, your response might be a bit more cautious. Also, even though cats look harmless, their claws are sharp. Cats sometimes bite, and they are unpredictable. How do you then help a child? (The following approach can be used with a number of other animals or fear objects as well.)

Instead of pushing the child toward his total fear, try gradual exposure. Show him pictures of a cat or point out the qualities of cats on the various ads on television. Let the child watch you demonstrate your joy in handling a cat. Let the child know that he can pet the cat as you do. Don't force him to do so, but when he does touch the cat, talk about how soft the cat's fur is, how pretty it is, etc. It is important to select a cat that is calm and one that responds positively to love and attention. Encourage the child to pet the cat with you more and more frequently. The time will come when the child is able to do this on his own and be spontaneous about it.

Some parents have found it helpful to have the child keep a written record of his progress regarding whatever it is that he fears or that upsets his life. Such a written record shows the child he is attaining a goal. For example, the record might indicate when the child responded to a cat, how long, where, and what his positive feelings were.

In addition to the fear of animals, **nighttime** fears — such as fear of the **dark** and of **nightmares** — are very common.

Darkness can be especially frightening to a child, for it generates a sense of feeling isolated, abandoned or lost. A gradual approach once again can be helpful. A child needs to know that it is all right to talk about his fears, that he will not be made fun of for being afraid. You might try gradually reducing the amount of light in the child's room. Share the following verse with the child and help him commit it to memory:

> When you lie down you shall not be afraid; yes, you
> shall lie down and your sleep shall be sweet. Be not

afraid of sudden terror and panic, nor of the stormy blast or the storm and ruin of the wicked when it comes [for you will be guiltless], for the Lord shall be your confidence, firm and strong, and shall keep your foot from being caught [in a trap or hidden danger] (Proverbs 3:24-26, *The Amplified Bible*).

Many children have nightmares or, as they call them, "bad dreams," three to six times a month. When you or I take a fear to bed with us it often crops up again in our dreams—our minds run wild during our sleep. So we realize that children's persistent and repetitive nightmares may indicate that excessive tension, stress or fear has been felt during their day. When their dreams occur nightly or several times a night, it may be telling you something. (For specific and detailed help with children's fears, see *Helping the Fearful Child*, by Dr. Jonathan Kellerman.[1])

To understand your child's fears and anxieties better, ask him what he thinks about when he is going to sleep at night. Ask him if he's ever afraid or if he ever worries. Read him the following poem and see how he responds.

WHATIF

Last night, while I lay thinking here,
Some Whatifs crawled inside my ear
And pranced and partied all night long
And sang their same old Whatif song:
Whatif I'm dumb in school?
Whatif they've closed the swimming pool?
Whatif I get beat up?
Whatif there's poison in my cup?
Whatif I flunk that test?
Whatif green hair grows on my chest?

Whatif nobody likes me?
Whatif a bolt of lightning strikes me?
Whatif I don't grow taller?
Whatif my head starts getting smaller?
Whatif the wind tears up my kite?
Whatif they start a war?
Whatif my parents get divorced?
Whatif the bus is late?
Whatif my teeth don't grow in straight?
Whatif I tear my pants?
Whatif I never learn to dance?
Everything seems swell, and then
The nighttime Whatifs strike again!

(Source unknown)

You might want to share with your child some of the worries you can remember having when you were young as a way to encourage your child to share his with you. You could make a game of it. Read a list of your own "whatifs" to your child and then ask your child what his "whatifs" are.

How We Can Help

Children learn most of their fears. This means that it is also possible for them to unlearn them. Dr. Kellerman suggests a number of practical and workable ways to help children rid their lives of fear:

1. Let the child know that *it is all right to be afraid*. Everyone has fears at some time in his life. A certain amount of fear is normal and we don't have to be ashamed when we are afraid. Share your own childhood fears and let the child know those fears passed from your life. This can be an encouragement to him.

2. Help the child understand that *being afraid*

is temporary. He may even fear that his fear will last forever. Children need a message of hope for the future.

3. Let the child know that *it is good to talk about his fear.* Sharing it helps him keep it in perspective and avoid distortions. His sharing will help you to know the extent of his fear, and then you are better equipped to help him overcome any distortions. Many parents have found it easier for the child when they have him draw his feelings or fears on a piece of paper with crayons, or act out his fantasies, or use puppets to talk out his fears.

4. Let the child know that *it is also normal not to be afraid.* When a child can observe another person not being afraid in a situation where he is fearful, he gets the message that it is possible not to be afraid.

5. Help the child learn that *a new behavior will replace his fear response.* These new responses are called counter behaviors or fear-replacing behaviors. Encourage the child to imagine himself not being afraid in his usual fear experience. These kinds of positive imageries are powerful substitutes which we could all use to greater effectiveness. Even encouraging a child to become angry in his fear situation can be beneficial. It is difficult to be both fearful and angry at the same time. The anger will give him a greater feeling of control. Participating in a positive activity or favorite pastime when the feared object or situation is at hand can eventually lessen the fear.

As with adults, so with children—repeated facing of a fear is the best method of overcoming it. We all need to use the creative powers of our God-given imagination to visualize ourselves handling the fearful event. Depending upon the comprehension level of the child, selected portions of Scripture will help bring peace and comfort to his mind.

One of the underlying themes of fear for both children and adults is the fear of the unknown. We desire certainty. We want to be assured that we will be all right, that we will be safe, that our questions will be answered, and that we will be able to do what we are asked to do.

Many of our other specific fears have their roots in this fear. However, though we may not know all that will happen, God does know. The psalmist says, "Thou knowest my downsitting and mine uprising, thou understandest my thought afar off" (Psalm 139:2, KJV).

One of the great lessons of life for a child is to come to the place where he can say, "It's all right for me not to know all the answers because I trust in God and He helps me handle life's uncertainties."

¤　　¤　　¤　　¤　　¤

Let me talk with you now about what may be one of *your* fears as a parent. You may be apprehensive about recognizing the fears in your children's lives.

Don't be too hard on yourself. Most of us received little or no training in how to be a parent before our children were born. And even if we had, our humanity would still show through. We are not all-knowing and there are no guarantees in parenting. God expects us to do our best, but He doesn't expect us to be perfect.

6

DEPRESSION

Depression is not a respecter of persons. It can be felt acutely by anyone of any age. It attacks adults, young adults and teenagers; even very young children often show signs of being depressed. Sometimes professional counseling is needed, but many times, simply by following the principles set forth in this chapter, a parent can help either a young child or a teenager through this difficult time.

Depression in Children

Perhaps it seems odd to discuss depression in young children as a problem, but we must be aware that it occurs much more often than we might imagine.

A child's depression often goes undetected by the adults around him. This condition in children is probably hidden more successfully than when it occurs in any other age group. The child doesn't realize he is depressed, and even if parents suspect that something is wrong, they often deny their child is chronically unhappy. They fail to recognize, accept or respond appropriately to the child's symptoms. After all, who wants to admit his child is depressed?

Recognizing the Symptoms

How can you recognize childhood depression? Here is a composite picture of how a child would appear if every characteristic of depression were included.

First of all, the child would appear quite *unhappy*. He would not verbally complain of this, and he might not even be aware of it, but his behavior would give you that impression.

This sad child also would demonstrate *withdrawal and inhibition*. His interest in normal activities would diminish. He would appear listless, and his parents would think he is bored or sick.

Often concerned parents begin looking for some symptoms of a hidden physical illness, and indeed some *physical symptoms* could further blur the earmarks of depression. These symptoms include headaches, stomach aches and sleeping or eating disturbances.

Discontent is a common mood. The child would give the impression of being dissatisfied. He would derive little pleasure from what he does. People often wonder if someone else is responsible for the way the child feels.

The child would feel *rejected and unloved*. He would tend to withdraw from anything that might be a disappointment to him. As with other age groups, a *negative self-concept* and even feelings of worthlessness would be present.

Irritability and a low frustration tolerance would be seen, but the child would be unaware of why he is upset.

Sometimes, however, he would act just the opposite, attempting to deal with his depressive feelings by *clowning around* and provoking others. He especially may act this way at a time of achievement because he would find it difficult to handle something positive. This provocative behavior makes other people angry.

Now of course, these characteristics will not all be present in every case of a depressed child. When several of them are obvious, though, or any one is particularly intense, depression should be suspected.

Sometimes children will experience and express their depression in the same way as adults, but not always. However, enlightened adults can recognize the symptoms fairly easily. Because of their limited experience and physiology, children tend to express their depression as rebellion, negativity, anger and resentment. The depression expressed when parents divorce, for example, may be manifested by bedwetting, attacking friends or siblings, clinging to parents, failure in school or exaggerated storytelling.

Looking for the Causes

Why do children become depressed? It could be caused by any of the following: a physical defect or illness; malfunction of the endocrine glands; lack of affection, which can create insecurity in the child; lack of positive feedback or encouragement for accomplishments; death of a parent; divorce, separation, or desertion by a parent; parental favor toward a sibling; poor relationship between the child and a step-parent; economic problems in the home; moving to a new home or school; punishment by others.[1]

Look for any type of loss that may have occurred in the child's life. This could be the loss of a pet or friend, a severe rejection experience, a divorce situation, or a death in the family. A child's thoughts and feelings due to the loss of a parent through divorce probably will be similar to and as intense as those experienced when there is a death. Whatever the type of loss, try to see it from the child's point of view. It is easy to misinterpret a child's perspective, especially if you have not been around children very much.

Differences Due to Child's Age

The signs and symptoms of depression vary with the child's age. Even infants can be depressed, and an infant who is depressed simply may not thrive. Generally, children age two to five are less apt to experience depression than those younger or older. However, a parent's moods may severely affect a small child. For example, a mother who is depressed may withdraw from her child, who in turn also becomes depressed. The problem is that the child usually cannot overcome his depression until the mother overcomes hers.

A Young Child

Depression in a young child is a normal reaction to a perceived loss, and you as the adult need to accept it as such, whatever the cause may be. Allow the child a period of time to adjust to the loss. Let your child know that everyone experiences sadness and depression at one time or another — but be sure to put it into terminology the child can understand. Explain that feelings like this are normal and that in time they will go away and the child will feel better. Encourage him to tell God about his feelings and assure him that God understands our down times as well as our happy times.

As a child goes through the adjustment process, keep in mind the characteristics of both the magic years of the younger child and the middle years of the older child. A child in either age group will need to:

—accept the pain of the loss;
—remember and review his relationship with the loved person;
—become familiar with all the different feelings that are part of grief: anger, sadness and despair;
—express to others his sorrow, anger and sense of loss;
—verbalize any feelings of guilt;
—find a network of caretakers. He needs many people to support him at this time.[2]

The younger child especially will need to be helped to experience the depression as fully as possible. Resisting or ignoring the depression merely prolongs the experience. Encourage the child to be as honest as possible in expressing his feelings, in admitting that he is depressed or sad, and listen without being judgmental or critical. He needs your support.

If grief is involved, you need to allow the child, no matter what his age, to do the grieving naturally. If the grief is over divorce, do not expect him to get over it quickly. This type can last a long time, and it can recur from time to time.

Help the child find some type of activity that will bolster him. A new game, a sight-seeing trip, or anything that would interest him may be helpful.

Find a way for the child to experience some type of success. Recall what he has done fairly well, and help him use that special ability again. His self-esteem can be rediscovered and elevated through small successes.

Help the child break out of his routine. Even such simple items as a new food at a meal or taking him to a special restaurant may help. Taking a day off for an outing may be particularly helpful.

A Teenager

John sits staring at the wall. He has been that way for several days. This last week he missed several of his classes, and when he did attend, he sat quietly with very little response. At dinner tonight he picked at his food and left most of it untouched. In fact, he hasn't even eaten with the rest of the family much recently. His friends have stopped calling since he turns down so many of their invitations. What is wrong? John is depressed.

What causes depression in teens? Mostly, the same things that cause depression in adults, with the transitional struggles of adolescence thrown in as well. Let's consider this concern since stress can be connected to depression.

A sense of loss is one of the major themes underlying depression, but it is often overlooked. Being rejected by someone, losing an athletic event, having to wear braces at sixteen, and so on, can be real losses to a teen, though adults may not perceive them as such.

There are other, more serious, losses. When a teen loses a parent in death, for example, he often denies the fact in order to protect himself from the threatening feelings of grief which accompany such a loss. If the relationship was close, there will be intense pain, and even anger at being left alone.

The death of a brother or sister can produce conflicting feelings because of the mixture of positive and negative feelings siblings usually have for one another.

If a teen loses a friend in death, there is intense anxiety. Teenagers are aware that adults die, but the death of a peer is shocking and unnerving. It forces a teen to face his own mortality at an age when he is not prepared to do so.

Another shock that many teens face is the loss of a parent through divorce. When this occurs, the teen loses his security and his confidence in the future. Anger at the parent who left usually is stronger and lasts longer than if the person had died. A teen thinks, *If he had died, he wouldn't have been able to help it. He wouldn't have had a choice. But it's only a divorce, and he had a choice. So why did he leave?*

A teen tends to blame himself to a large degree for his parents' divorce, and the guilt he feels over the part he thinks he played is strong—and difficult to resolve.

Even when a friend moves away, the teen experiences a deep sense of loss. The same sense of loss can occur when the teen himself has to change schools or make some other type of move.[3]

Another factor to consider is that the normal developmental process itself presents teenagers with a number of real losses and threats to their self-esteem. During this time they are expected to loosen their dependence upon their parents. Some are tied closer to Mom and Dad than others and are hesitant to do this, whereas others may break away as fast as they can.

They are also expected to take responsibility for their future and eventually the running of their own lives. Learning to live without some of the previous sources of gratification can be an underlying factor for depression.

A sudden loss can create in a teen the sense of being out of control and of floundering. A loss that is gradual, even though it may be painful, can be prepared for, at least to some degree.

Often the depression is heightened if what is lost is seen by the teen as necessary and irreplaceable. In his book on counseling the depressed, Archibald Hart, dean of the graduate school of psychology at Fuller Seminary, describes four different types of losses:

Abstract losses are intangible, such as the loss of self-respect, love, hope or ambition. Our minds perceive these losses, and we feel we have experienced them. At times the loss may be real, but it may not be as bad as we feel it is.

Concrete losses involve tangible objects—a home, a car, a parent, a close friend, a photograph or a pet. We could feel and see the object prior to the loss.

Imagined losses are created solely by our active imaginations. We think someone doesn't like us anymore. We think people are talking behind our backs. Teens often excel at this. Their self-talk focuses on negatives and may not be based on fact.

The most difficult type of loss to handle, however, is the *threatened loss*. This loss has not yet occurred, but there is the real possibility that it will happen. To a teen, waiting for the results of a physical exam or waiting to hear from the admissions office of a college to which he has applied carries the possibility of loss. Depression occurs because, in this type of loss, the teen is powerless to do anything about it. In a sense, he is immobilized.

The Younger Teen

There is a difference between the depression of teens aged thirteen through sixteen or seventeen and that of older adolescents. A young teen will avoid admitting personal concerns and may not exhibit or even experience the hopelessness or self-depreciation adults or older teens feel. A young teen is oriented less to *thinking* about something than *doing* something, and is apt to express or handle depression in one of these three different ways:

1. He will *deny* internal depression, but it can be recognized by excessive fatigue, even after adequate rest; hypochondria (an abnormal concern about normal physical changes going on within him); or an inability to concentrate in school or in other situations.

2. He may be *keeping too busy* in an attempt to keep his mind off of things. He may demonstrate an unnatural need to be with people, or he may prefer to be alone, pursuing his own private activities with tremendous intensity.

3. He may consciously or subconsciously appeal for help through *unacceptable behavior,* which can include tempter tantrums, running away, stealing, or a variety of other rebellious acts. These are usually conducted in such a manner as to ensure his being caught.[4]

The Older Teen

An older teen tends to manifest his depression in ways similar to those of adults. Yet he may still express it indirectly, through maladaptive behavior. How?

Drug use is one means of expression. It helps the

young person defend himself against being depressed. The secrecy of obtaining illegal drugs can add excitement to his life, and sharing the drug experience offers peer relationships.

Sexual promiscuity also is used as a defense against depression, more frequently by girls than boys. They believe that the attention and the feeling of being needed and wanted can overcome their sadness and their loneliness.

Suicidal behavior is another clear manifestation. There has been a significant rise in suicidal behavior and even in actual accomplished suicide among both early and later teens. It may be a reflection of depression, or it could be tied in with other causes, but the family of a depressed teen should be aware of the possibility.

DANGER SIGNALS OF SUICIDE[5]

Suicide is a topic we would all prefer to avoid — but we cannot, especially when we see the increase in the number of adolescent suicides. Every 83 minutes a teenager commits suicide in our country. Those are just the ones we know about.

Each year, the reported cases of attempted suicides for teens is more than 500,000. It is the third major cause of death for adolescents. Sometimes the stress and futility of life (even for Christian youth) seems overwhelming to them and this seems the only answer. When a teen experiences depression, the causes may not be clear to him or to us; thus, there is no clear solution.

Even though most parents are shocked when their teen commits suicide or even makes an attempt to, in retrospect they realize there were warning signs. It is important to take any hint or indication concerning suicide seriously. Here are some danger signals which may help

Guidelines for Helping Depressed Kids

What can you say to your child or teen who is going through depression?

For openers, you can simply say, "I care for you and am available. I want to be with you."

There is healing in the physical touch. An arm around the shoulder, a pat on the back, or taking hold of the hand all convey acceptance. Be honest and tell your child, "I don't understand all that you are going through, but I am trying—and I'm here to help you."

Most people don't know what to do for their depressed kids. Here are some practical guidelines. How closely you follow these will depend upon the intensity and duration of the depression. If it is only for a few hours or a day or two, or if the person is feeling

---

you recognize it if this problem ever arises:

- Often a teen becomes preoccupied with death themes, or expresses suicidal thoughts.

- Sometimes the person will give away prized possessions. He may even make a will or make some other type of final arrangements.

- Severe changes in sleeping habits could be a sign.

- Sudden and extreme changes in eating habits and weight could be a clue.

- Any changes in school attendance or grades, or dropping out of favorite activities, may be a clue.

- Watch for personality changes such as nervousness, outbursts of anger, or apathy regarding health or appearance.

- Use of drugs or alcohol should arouse your suspicions.

down but is still functioning, not all of the suggestions would apply. However, if the depression has lasted for quite a while, and the child is dragging around, not functioning, not eating, or not sleeping, you should apply the appropriate measures.

1. *Understand the causes and symptoms of depression.* If your child is so depressed that he just stares, ignores greetings, or turns away from you, remember that he doesn't want to act that way. In depression, the person loses the ability to govern his thinking and his emotions. If he is severely depressed, he cannot control himself any more than you could walk a straight line after twirling yourself around twenty-five times. Understanding the normal behavior of a depressed person will enable you to control your own responses better and you will be able to help your child more effectively.

- A recent suicide of a friend, relative or admired public figure could be cause for concern if your teen has a weak formation of his own identity. He may identify too much with the deceased and try to follow that person's lead.

- Any previous suicide attempt is serious since the next attempt usually occurs within three months.

- Some teens talk about obtaining guns, knives or other weapons.

- A loss of interest in friends or peers may be significant, especially if it continues.

- Watch out for verbal inuendos such as: "You won't have to worry about me for very long"; or, "I won't bother you anymore"; or, "Maybe it would be better if I were dead"; or, "You'll be sorry. Just wait and see."

If any of these danger signals continue, be alert. You may need to seek professional help.

---

2. *Watch out for the possibility of suicide, even with children.* If you even suspect your child may be thinking along this line, take it very seriously. Unfortunately, this tragic problem is on the increase. The family of any depressed person should be aware of the potential of suicide. Realize that any individual who is so depressed that he talks about the utter hopelessness of the future might be considering ending his own life. Every hint or statement or allusion to suicide should be talked about. Ask the child to tell you about his suicidal thoughts or plans. It helps the depressed person if the subject can be brought out into the open. Then he knows that other people are aware and can be called upon for help and support.

3. *Get the depressed child or teen to a doctor if the condition continues.* Your family physician may be able to help, or he may recommend someone who can. The time factor is very important. Don't let depression go on and on. For a teen, you may have to make the arrangements, guide him firmly into the car, and just go!

As long as you tolerate a child or a teen's depression, you help maintain it.

4. *Give the child your full support but don't overreact.* The entire family needs to be made aware of the situation and instructed as to their responses. Confrontation with a depressed teen and strong discipline with a child should be suspended until they achieve greater stability. Ask the family not to attack the person, not to bring up his failures, not to come down hard on him, and not to ask him to do things he is not capable of doing while he is depressed.

5. *Don't avoid the depressed child or teen.* He doesn't have the plague. Avoidance further isolates him and could make him feel worse. You might be avoiding

him because you feel guilty about his depression, thinking you are the cause. Be aware that one person may contribute to another's problem from time to time, but no one person is responsible for another's happiness.

6. *Understand that a depressed child or teen really hurts.* It may be even worse for the younger child since it's hard for him to understand why he feels so bad. Don't suggest to either one that he does not really feel bad or that he is just trying to get your sympathy. Don't tell him to "snap out of it." Don't tell him that all he has to do is "just pray to God about it," or "read the Word more," giving him the impression that any of those actions will solve everything.

Often a depressed person deliberately chooses portions of Scripture that reinforce his feelings of loss and unworthiness. Any Scriptures given to a depressed person must be selected with care.

7. *Empathize, rather than sympathize, with your child or teen.* Sympathy can only reinforce a person's feelings of hopelessness. It may make him feel even more helpless and may lower his already low self-esteem. Statements such as, "It's so awful that you are depressed"; or, "You must feel miserable"; or, "How could this ever happen?" rarely help.

8. *Make sure he eats.* If he doesn't want to eat, you can say, "Look, you may not feel like eating, but you probably are hungry. Starving won't help. Food is important, so let's eat now. I'll sit down and eat with you, and then let's talk about what's troubling you."

Don't harp on the food problem, though, or on his eating habits. Saying, "You'll make me feel bad if you don't eat this food"; or, "Think of all the starving people in China," won't get him to eat. Instead, it will probably make him feel worse. Remember, not eating is a symptom of being depressed.

9. *Keep the person busy.* This is one of the best things you can do for him. Physical activity during severe depression can be more beneficial than mental activity.

The activities planned should be those that he has enjoyed in the past, with all preparations made in detail. If he has lost interest in those activities, gently remind him of the fun he had before with them and then firmly and positively insist that he become involved. Don't ask him if he would like to, because he might not know, or he may not care to respond. Don't get angry and say, "You're going with me because I'm sick and tired of you sitting around feeling sorry for yourself." Rather, you could say, "I know you haven't been feeling well, but you are entitled to some enjoyment. I think you might like this once we get started. And I would like to share this activity with you."

Perhaps you could call to find out what time a school game or activity begins. Upon hanging up you say to your teen or child, "I think we can get ready for it, so let's start now." If you are going shopping, you could suggest, "Come along. I like to have someone with me, and I need your advice."

Any activity can be used, but be aware that you may need to schedule his entire day for him. By getting him involved, you can help him begin to break destructive behavior patterns, and this helps him gain energy and motivation.

10. *Don't ever tease your child or teen, or lecture him, about his lack of confidence.* However, don't ignore it either. Loss of self-esteem is common in depression, and it must be faced. In reactivating confidence, help the child see the lack of logic of his self-disparagement,

but don't do it by berating or arguing. Also, don't join in his self-pity. Rather, look for past accomplishments and get him to focus on what he was able to do. You can say, "Perhaps you can't do some things the way you did before, but let's talk about the things you still do well. What do you think they are?"

If he says, "I can't do anything," gently name something he can do, or try to draw it out of him. At this point you are trying to help him overcome his sense of helplessness.

Be persistent and steady in your responses to the child's depression. Remember that, at this point, you have more control over your emotional responses than he has over his.

If the depression is severe and the child does not respond, he should have professional help. However, a parent can help a child handle many depressive experiences without taking him for counseling. By following these principles, you will be much more able to fulfill the biblical teaching on giving empathy and encouragement, and you will be guiding your child toward a considerably more positive attitude toward life.

> Bear one another's burdens, and thus fulfill the law of Christ (Galatians 6:2).

> Therefore encourage one another, and build up one another, just as you also are doing (1 Thessalonians 5:11).

DIVORCE

One of the most stressful things that happens to children is the divorce of their parents. That can be the most traumatic experience a child will ever have to face.

Newsweek magazine has estimated that 45 percent of all children will live with only one parent at some time before they are eighteen. Twelve million children now under the age of eighteen have parents who are divorced.

The effects of divorce on children have been shown to be more serious and longer lasting than many divorced parents are willing to admit. Studies released in England in 1978 showed that children of divorce have a shorter life expectancy and more illness than those in families where no divorce occurred. These children leave school earlier as well In New York City, which has a very high adolescent suicide rate, two of every three teenage suicides involve teenagers whose parents are divorced. Many other teens carry a pattern of insecurity, depression anxiety, and anger into their adult years.[1] On the average it takes a child up to five years to adjust to the impact of his parents' divorce.[2]

What a Child Loses

In a divorce, children experience many losses. These can include not only the loss of one of the parents, but also the loss of home, neighborhood, school friends, family standard of living, family outings, family holiday get-togethers, and so on.

A child's self-esteem is in serious jeopardy, too. Have you ever wondered what it would be like to learn, as a child, that your parents are divorcing, feel the panic of it, and then have to face telling your friends? Fear becomes a daily companion, and the losses multiply.

When a child loses a parent, he also may lose his hope for the future. Because of the uncertainty, a child can feel out of control to a greater extent than ever before. The parents upon whom he depended are no longer the solid rock he needs, and the shakiness of his situation can soon show up in such areas as family finances. If a divorced father has promised to take care of the family and his monthly payments become irregular, and then eventually cease, the child's uncertainty becomes more acute—and what emotional loss must he feel regarding his father's apparent lack of concern for him? This is an additional stressor.

How Age Affects Reactions

Divorce affects children in different ways depending upon the age of the child.

Young children of *three to five,* and even younger,

become fearful; the routine separations of life become traumatic. A parent's going shopping or the child's leaving for preschool is a stressful experience.

These children tend to regress to earlier behavior patterns and become more passive and dependent. More and more they ask questions like, "What's that?" in an effort to overcome the disorganization of the crisis. They have a great need for affection. They may refuse to feed themselves, and some even revert to a need for diapers. They can create wild and imaginative fantasies in their minds because they are puzzled by what is happening to them. They are bewildered. Play does not have the same sense of fun. These preschoolers may become aggressive with other children.

In addition, some psychologists believe that the absence of a parent of the opposite sex could be damaging to the child's sexual development. A child learns about sexuality and male/female responses by observing the interaction between his mother and father. A positive role model helps create the image of how he or she is to respond in the future.

For example, the first man in a girl's life is her father. Through his interactions, she learns how to respond to men in her life. A healthy, positive relationship helps her obtain the balance she needs. If Father is either absent or a "phantom father" (he is there but uninvolved), she may develop a fear response toward men or become over-involved with every man she encounters. (For more information on this topic, see *Always Daddy's Girl* by this author.[3])

On the other side, I have talked with men who were raised without a mother or sisters and as a result were at a loss in being able to develop healthy relationships with women in their own lives.

When you are counseling a three- to five-year-old child whose parents are divorcing, help the child verbalize his hurt and his idea of why his parents are divorcing. Throughout all the stages of childhood, a common thought is, *Did I cause my parent's divorce? Am I responsible for not having a family any more?* As we mentioned before, a child this young has unrealistic perceptions and may feel as though his behavior or thoughts actually caused the divorce. It is not easy to convince him otherwise, but it is vital to try to help him see other possibilities.

The *six- to eight-year-old* has his own set of reactions. Sadness is there, and his sense of responsibility for the parents' breakup is stronger. His feelings of loss are deep. He is afraid of being abandoned, and sometimes even of starving. He yearns for the parent who has left.

Frequently these children are angry with the parent who cares for them all the time. They have conflicting loyalties. They want to love both parents, but they struggle with the feeling that loving one is being disloyal to the other. Thus they feel torn and confused. Symptoms can include nail biting, bedwetting, loss of sleep, and retreating into fantasy to solve family problems. Children of both age groups become possessive.

Preadolescent children of *nine to twelve* usually experience anger as their main emotional reaction. This anger is felt toward the one the child feels is responsible for the family breakup, who could be the custodial parent. However, instead of leveling his anger directly at the parent, he may aim it at his peers, alienating them at the time he needs them most.

The child of this age also suffers from a badly

shaken self-image. Some of these children will throw themselves into what they are doing with great intensity as their way of combatting that and of handling the disruption of their lives.

Teens, when a divorce occurs, respond largely on the basis of their own personalities and weaknesses which have already developed. If their home is no longer a safe retreat, they may tend to spend more and more time away. They may feel pressured to mature too rapidly and take on adult responsibilities or behaviors before they are ready. Because of this, some may rebel with childish behavior. If parental supervision is inadequate, they can get into real trouble.

When their parents begin to date again, teens may feel threatened since this brings into focus the fact that their parents are sexual beings and have their own set of needs. If a parent is upset, a teen may want to help but not know how. Or a parent could dump his or her frustration and upset upon the teen who is not capable of dealing with these adult issues.

The normal concerns of teens intensify because their world is shattered—and what happens to the values they have been taught? Most parents teach their children that marriage is for life—and now they are divorced. You can see why a teen would be confused and disillusioned.

A Child's Two Main Concerns

In the turmoil of divorce, children of all ages have two major concerns.

The **first** is their *dream that their parents will reconcile.* The children believe that if this were to happen, all their problems would be over. They think that, in spite of previous problems, the family was better off when both parents were there. The child may have seen the conflict, but he is willing to tolerate it in order to have an intact family. After all, this is the only family he knows.

His **second** concern revolves around himself— *what will happen to him?* He is afraid that the parent he is living with will abandon him. One parent already did. Why shouldn't the other?

If one parent was forced to leave (as many are), the child's fear centers on being thrown out as his mother or father was. Again this is a stressor.

Another fear concerns being replaced in the parents' affection by someone else. As the custodial parent begins to date, the child wonders if this new person is going to become important to his parent. If so, will he lose the time and attention he now receives?

Emotional Stages of Reaction

In order to help the child of a divorced couple, it is important to understand what he experiences. Remember that his feelings will change with the passage of time. There are fairly clear emotional stages through which a child passes as he struggles to understand and deal with a divorce. These stages are normal, and they cannot be avoided or bypassed. They have nothing to do with the spirituality of the child. Your goal, in endeavoring to help the child, is to guide him as he passes through these stages in order to minimize the negative effects and produce positive growth.

Shock. Although a child's home may be filled with visible conflict, the child rarely expects his parents to get a divorce. He may not like the conflict, but he hopes it will settle down eventually. Discovering that a separation or divorce is going to happen is usually a great shock to a child.

Fear and anxiety. These unsettling emotions will occur because the child is now faced with an unknown future. In the past a home and family with two parents have been the child's source of stability. Those are now about to be shattered.

Fear and anxiety may manifest themselves in restlessness, nightmares, sleeplessness, stomach problems, sweating, and aches and pains. These are normal problems. A child needs to be given reassurance. It is important to give him the facts, because a child's imagination may run wild, and knowing is better than wondering. A child may tend to think up worse problems than actually exist.

Feeling abandoned and rejected. After fear and anxiety come feelings of abandonment and rejection. The feelings of the initial stage recede and are replaced by this struggle. The child may know at one level that he will not be rejected or abandoned, but at a deeper level he is still concerned that it might happen. A younger child has difficulty distinguishing between the parents leaving one another and their leaving him, and he may focus on this. This stage of the child's emotions may be perpetuated by unkept promises on the part of the parent who leaves.

Loneliness and sadness. Feeling sad and alone soon replaces the sense of abandonment and rejection. As the family structure changes and calms down, the reality of what has occurred begins to settle in. A child sometimes feels this stage with a pain in the stomach and a tightness in the chest. This is when depression begins and regular activities tend to be neglected. Many children do a lot of thinking, which is usually wishful daydreaming. These fantasies follow the same theme—parents get together again and everything is all right. Crying spells may become more frequent at this time.

Frustration and anger. These feelings are the next to come—children whose parents divorce or separate become angry children. This is a natural response to the frustrations they feel. In addition, they have seen upset and angry parents, and the children emulate this modeling of anger. The anger may continue to be the pattern for many years and, unless dealt with and resolved, probably will carry over into adult relationships.

The child's anger is there for several reasons. It serves as a protection and a warning signal, just like depression. It is often a reaction to hurt, fear or frustration, and it alerts others to the fact that there is a problem.

The anger may not show itself directly. It's an inner, basic feeling which, rather than being expressed openly, may be suppressed or masked. It may become evident, then, through a negative perspective on life, or through irritability, or withdrawal and self-isolation. Anger also may be expressed through strong resistance—to school, or chores, or whatever the child wants to resist.

Anger is an involuntary response, so don't be threatened by it or attempt to deny its presence in the child. Rather, help the child learn to express and drain it. According to his ability, help him to understand the cause for his anger, and its purpose. If it is not allowed a direct expression, it can come out in an indirect manner, and may erupt in violence. This exhibition would indicate displaced anger and is far more dangerous than allowing a child to acknowledge his anger and speak openly about it.

Resentment and rejection (by the child). Eventually the child's anger moves to resentment and results in his doing the rejecting. He is not over his angry feelings but is now attempting to create some emotional distance between himself and his parent. This is a protective device. Pouting can be one of his forms of rejection, as can the silent treatment. The child won't respond to suggestions or commands, and he often "forgets" to follow through with what he is supposed to do. He becomes hypercritical as well.

This behavior is actually a reaction formation. As a child pushes a parent away, he really wants to be close to the parent. He makes hateful statements and yet wants to be loving. He is trying to protect himself from being rejected, so he rejects first.

Reestablishing trust. The final stage for a child in the problem of dealing with parental divorce is the reestablishment of trust. It is difficult to say how long this will take, as it varies with each situation and child, and can range from months to years.

Helping Your Kids Through These Stages

What can parents or adults do to help? Here are some suggestions:

1. Do not be so concerned with your own feelings that you neglect the child's feelings. Give him some time each day to discuss what he is experiencing and feeling.

2. Allow the child time to process his feelings. There are no quick solutions or cures.

3. A stable environment is beneficial to the child no matter what his age. It's better for him not to have

to move but to live with his remaining parent in the same home and neighborhood with as many things as possible staying the same. Of course, some change will be necessary, and the child will need to adapt, but the parent must realize that the greater the change, the greater the stress and discomfort to the child or teen.

4. Give positive feedback to the child, and build his sense of self-confidence.

5. Reassure him that he is not the cause of the divorce or separation. Both parents need to give him consistent and equal amounts of love.

6. According to the child's level of understanding, help him to know in advance the different types of feelings he will be experiencing. Keep the child informed at all times of any environmental changes expected so he can be prepared.

A child needs to be assured that even though his mother and father will be working through their own struggles as the divorce proceeds, they still will be taking care of him. Parents, friends, and other relatives need to repeat this to the child often so he begins to realize that more than one person is supporting him with this belief. This is an especially appropriate time to assist the child to select some interesting task he can accomplish that will help him overcome his feelings of helplessness and of being out of control.[4]

Blended Families

Some people see remarriage as an answer to their difficulties. Unfortunately, blended families have their own style of stresses and problems. It appears that infants and young children make blended family adjustments a bit easier than teens. It's important to realize that even though you may see your teenager "changing," a teen thrives on stability and sameness. For example, could you listen to the same record day in and day out for twenty weeks? He does.

In most divorces a teen sees what happened as a personal rejection. Because of this he or she has learned to close up—and then, when the parent remarries, he is expected to open up!

A teen involved in the remarriage of a parent has a number of questions. Some of them are:

"How often will I see my real parent now?"

"Will my real parent feel that I have 'sold out' if I show positive feelings toward my new stepparent?"

"Why do I have to share my real mom or dad with these other kids who have invaded my home?"

"Why can't I have as much time with my own parent as I did when there was no stepparent around?"

Many come to the conclusion that life is not fair, and they can't wait to get old enough to leave home. A blended family often brings more new losses for a teen than it does gains.

One stress experienced particularly by teens is brought about by grieving over the parent who leaves and then facing the problem of divided loyalties. Teens value loyalty, so to love or care about a stepparent could seem disloyal to the teen. Teens need time to express their feelings and should be encouraged to do so. A blended family works best when expectations, fears, concerns and even resentments are anticipated and dealt with prior to the remarriage.

¤¤¤ **8** ¤¤¤

HELPING CHILDREN HANDLE THEIR STRESS

F̲or adults, teens, and children alike, stressors are a part of daily life and we don't worry about most of them. When a child breaks a finger, we have it set and assume it will heal. With chicken pox, we wait for him to get well. When he has a cold, we know he will recover.

When a child has an ulcer, however, or excessive fatigue, or a psychosomatic illness, that's a different matter. It's not so easy to deal with these conditions—which are caused by stress.

Four Ways of Coping

How do children approach life's stressors? They basically follow the same pattern we adults follow. There are four main ways in which we all try to cope:

1. We attempt to remove the stressor.
2. We decide to refuse to allow neutral situations to become stressors.
3. We try to deal directly with the stressor.
4. We look for ways of relaxing to ease the tension of the stress.

Both adults and children use these methods every day. Let's look a little more closely at each method as it relates to a child.

1. We attempt to remove the stressor.

Can a child *remove a stressor?* Occasionally, but usually he doesn't have the necessary power or control. In fact, children often are stuck—with no hope of removal—in a situation which becomes a source of intense stress, so they deal with it by inventing means of getting out of its way. A child may give up his friends because their behavior either is contrary to his standards or it is frightening to him—or both. Or, during a family fight he may go to his room and turn up his radio to drown out the noise.

2. We decide to refuse to allow neutral situations to become stressors.

As for *neutral situations* in a child's life, they sometimes get turned into stressors by other people. Exams at school are a case in point. They can be the source of acceptance or rejection by significant adults such as the child's teachers or parents. Some children worry about the exam, whereas other children refuse to let it pressure them by making statements to themselves like, "Why shouldn't I get a fairly good grade? I've studied and I've done all right so far. And even if I don't, it isn't the end of the world. I'm still okay."

3. *We try to deal directly with the stressor.*

What about *confronting a stressor* head-on and dealing directly with it? That may take figuring out a way to get around it. A child who is tired of being kidded about being heavy can go on a diet and lose weight. I saw a child in a class go to a teacher and ask to have his seat moved because he talked too much to his friend who sat next to him, and he was tired of getting into trouble for it.

4. *We look for ways of relaxing to ease
the tension of the stress.*

What about *relaxation?* How can children find a way to ease the tension when stress is facing them? How do *you* relax? Do you jog, play tennis, run, read a novel? These hobbies and activities which give us enjoyment are a source of relaxation for us.

Have you taken your child to the public library and introduced him to the wealth of material found on the shelves? Learning to read novels at an early age may provide one source of relaxation for him. You can help him find others.

Unfortunately, we often structure our children's activities so strictly that they have little time just to be kids. After-school sports are often overly competitive with an emphasis upon winning instead of on the enjoyment of the activity. We adults tend to be result-oriented rather than to do things just for the joy of it, and we project that philosophy onto our children. Yet the child needs a model in relaxation from us. Tim Hansel's book *When I Relax I Feel Guilty*[1] will assist you in helping your child find some good ways to relax.

Many children feel just what this little poem reflects:

I wish I was a rock, a-settin' on a hill;
I wasn't doin' nothin' but just a-settin' still.
I wouldn't eat; I wouldn't sleep;
I wouldn't even wash.
Just set there for a thousand years or so
And rest myself, by gosh!

(Source unknown)

To consider further those four ways of handling stress, answer each of the four questions in the first list below. Then ask your child to answer the next list of questions.

1. How do you see your child removing stressors in his or her life?
2. How do you see your child refusing to allow neutral situations to become stressors?
3. How do you see your child dealing directly with stressors?
4. How do you see your child relaxing?

Now ask your child:

1. How do you handle upsets and frustrations?
2. How do you refuse to let some problems upset you?
3. How do you handle a problem head-on?
4. What's the best way for you to relax?

(You may have to change the wording of some of these, depending upon the age of your child.)

Helping Children Learn

How can we help our children learn to handle the stressors of today more successfully?

One of the best descriptions I have heard of helping a young child is that it is like working on a jigsaw puzzle. You ask him to find the pieces; you point some of them out, and you help him fit the pieces together.

Here are some practical things you can observe as you attempt to help your child cope with the disappointments and stresses in his life.

As an adult, you need to *use the child's language* and be flexible in your communication. You must actively guide your conversation with a young child or you will end up failing to communicate. In working with your child, you need to make your statements very clear and even rephrase them several times. Repeat and repeat patiently. What may be clear to you simply may not register with your child.

Young children have one-track minds, often focusing on one aspect of an event to the exclusion of all others. They cannot see the forest for the trees. If you throw too much information and too many events at a child in one conversation, he cannot handle it. You need to *introduce other aspects of the situation gradually* as he is ready to take them on. Your task is to help the child see all the aspects, organize his thoughts, and explore other possible reasons for the stressful situation.

Whenever you try to help a young child, *remember these facts:* The child feels responsible for what has happened to initiate the stress; he makes connections different from the ones you make; he is egocentric; he has unrealistic and immature perceptions.

If this is how children think, what can you as a parent or teacher do to help this child who is under stress? Sometimes it will be impossible to fully change the child's pattern of thinking. You need to accept this as a fact of life and lessen your own frustration. *Helping a child fully express his inner thoughts and feelings* is one of the best approaches. It helps him gain greater self-control in a crisis event. By expressing his thoughts aloud, he can move to a new position. Patiently repeat your questions to the child, and encourage him to think aloud. Help him uncover the real or most probable reason for what is occurring. Try to help him discover this himself instead of giving him the reason. Look for any indications of guilt he may be experiencing.

A child needs time alone with his parent each week. This can be difficult if there are several children in the family, but it is needed. Parents need to be good listeners and help their child express his feelings, which in turn will help resolve his anger and frustrations. One of the best ways a child learns to handle stress is through observation within the home whether the family consists of both parents, one parent and a dog, grandparents, or those in a foster home. The positive attitude and modeling of the important adults in a child's life will give the child a firm foundation for dealing with the stresses of his life. (Since I am assuming that you are an adult reading this book, let me suggest two additional resources for your own reading: *Less Stress* by Dave and Jan Congo;[2] and my book, *How to Have a Creative Crisis.*[3] In this latter book, see the chapter on the questions of life.)

Children Who Cope

Children who are able to cope with the stressors of life accept their strengths and their limitations. They are also individualistic. They respond to peers, and they have a number of friends, but they still maintain their own individual identity.

In contrast, peer-oriented children are less sure of themselves and have a lower opinion of themselves.

Because peer pressure becomes so influential during adolescent years, preadolescent children must become aware of and able to maintain their own identity.

Children who cope are able to express their feelings. They can share their hopes, anger, hurts, frustrations and joys. They don't bottle up their feelings.[4]

If your child struggles with this, sit down with him, listen to his feelings of disappointment, and work with him on the alternatives. You may want to come up with a few suggestions including the ridiculous as well as the serious.

One eight-year-old boy wanted to do something, and he was disappointed and upset because he couldn't. His mother said, "I know five different ways you can handle this disappointment, Billy, and some of them may work. If you want to hear them, let me know."

In ten minutes he was back, asking.

"You really want to know?" his mother asked.

Billy grumbled and said, "Yes."

"Well," she said, "here they are. Maybe some are all right and maybe some aren't." She sat down with him and shared the following:

1. "I could go to my room and throw my clothes out the window to show everyone I'm upset."

2. "I could write a letter to God telling Him how disappointed I am and then read it to a friend."

3. "I could call eleven of my friends and complain to each of them."

4. "I could set the timer on the clock and cry for forty minutes until the bell rings."

5. "I could tell my mom that I'm disappointed and then we could talk about what we could do in-

stead and maybe plan for this activity another time."

This mother and son ended up with a very interesting discussion.

Like some adults, some children are not overly affected by the stressors of life. Why? Which children seem to handle the stressors of life best? They all seem to have some of the same characteristics.

- They can concentrate instead of jumping around from one thing to another.

- They can handle frustration.

- They can work at a job until it is finished.

- They have learned to accept the disappointments of life, or they find alternatives.

- They are able to postpone gratification. This is an important key. The children who handle stress well are those who can wait.

The Word of God

In addition to what we have discussed before, helping a child understand, commit to memory, and apply significant passages from the Word of God to his life is probably the most effective solution to stress.

A few of the passages which can become a source of stability and comfort to a child are:

James 1:2,3—Consider it all joy, my brethren, when you encounter various trials, knowing that the testing of your faith produces endurance.

Philippians 4:6-9—Be anxious for nothing, but in everything by prayer and supplication with thanksgiving let your requests be made known to God.

And the peace of God, which surpasses all comprehension, shall guard your hearts and your minds in Christ Jesus.

Finally, brethren, whatever is true, whatever is honorable, whatever is right, whatever is pure, whatever is lovely, whatever is of good repute, if there is any excellence and if anything worthy of praise, let your mind dwell on these things. The things you have learned and received and heard and seen in me, practice these things; and the God of peace shall be with you.

Psalm 37:1-9 — Do not fret because of evildoers.
Be not envious toward wrongdoers.
For they will wither quickly like the grass,
And fade like the green herb.
Trust in the LORD, and do good;
Dwell in the land and cultivate faithfulness.
Delight yourself in the LORD;
And He will give you the desires of your heart,
Commit your way to the LORD.
Trust also in Him, and He will do it.
And He will bring forth your righteousness as
    the light,
And your judgment as the noonday.
Rest in the LORD and wait patiently for Him;
Do not fret because of him who prospers in his way,
Because of the man who carries out wicked
    schemes.
Cease from anger, and forsake wrath;
Do not fret, it leads only to evildoing.
For evildoers will be cut off,
But those who wait for the LORD, they will inherit
    the land.

1 Peter 5:7—Casting all your anxiety upon Him, because He cares for you.

Isaiah 41:10,13—Do not fear, for I am with you;
Do not anxiously look about you, for I am your God.
I will strengthen you, surely I will help you.
Surely I will uphold you with My righteous right
    hand. . . .
For I am the LORD your God, who upholds your
    right hand,
Who says to you, "Do not fear, I will help you."

Psalm 27:1—The LORD is my light and my salvation; Whom shall I fear?
The LORD is the defense of my life;
Whom shall I dread?

Isaiah 26:3—The steadfast of mind Thou wilt keep
    in perfect peace, Because he trusts in Thee.

Psalm 4:8—In peace I will both lie down and sleep,
For Thou alone, O LORD, dost make me to dwell in
    safety.

Hebrews 13:6—The Lord is my helper, I will not be
    afraid. What shall man do to me?

Read these verses again. Write out how you would explain the meaning of each verse to a child. How would you help that child apply the passage to his own situation?

The child will learn best by seeing the reality of these passages lived out in the life of another individual. He needs to see the powerful effect of Scripture, and he needs to see that it does make a difference when a person puts into practice what God's Word has to say.

¤¤¤ **9** ¤¤¤

HELPING TEENS HANDLE THEIR STRESS

For teens, frustrations come in many packages, large and small. They're frustrated (and then stressed) by being thwarted, blocked, disappointed, etc. If they're hungry and can't eat, they get frustrated. If they want to join an elite club at school and are unable to do so, they become frustrated. If they try to untangle the mixed messages they receive about sex, they become frustrated.

Stress and Self-Talk

But do you really know why they get frustrated? It's because they have not learned to handle life when it doesn't go their way. Often they say, "Boy, do I want that," when in reality they are thinking, *I must have that. I've got to have it or my whole world will crumble. If I don't get it, the result will be total disaster. I've got to have my way!* This can include anything—a grade on an exam, making the team, having a pimple clear up before a date, having hair turn out right, etc. The list is endless. Many teens have not learned to say, "Boy, I really want that—but if I don't get it, it's not the end of the world. I may be disappointed and feel down for a while, but it's not going to cripple me. I can adjust and live without it and move ahead."

Much of the time our frustrations and stresses occur because of what we say to ourselves. This is called self-talk. All of us, children, teens and adults alike, talk to ourselves. When a teen learns to change his self-talk and his ways of responding when frustrated, he will experience less stress.

A person's perceptions and evaluations of the world around him as they relate to his own self-confidence actually can cause stress. Changing self-talk may be difficult but it also may be the best way to reduce stress, tension and anxiety.

Giving It Permission

One of the most important strategies for handling frustration and stress with self-talk is to give the situation permission to happen. When you resist something that is inevitable, it just persists and you become upset. Listen to this interaction between one parent and his teen:

JOHN: I was so upset today, I couldn't even think straight during my last two classes. I am really bummed out.

DAD: What happened? Do you want to tell me about it?

JOHN: I took most of my lunch hour to wait in line for those tickets we need, and after a half hour,

they closed the window and said there were no
more. And since I waited I was late for my next
class.

John went on sharing his frustration and after a
while his dad said, "How do you feel about your reaction to what happened? I can understand how that can
be frustrating, but what do you think now?"

JOHN: I wish it hadn't happened and I wish I
hadn't gotten so upset.

DAD: Want a wild suggestion?

JOHN: Well, it couldn't be any worse than what I
went through.

DAD: There was nothing you could do to control
what happened or to stop it, was there?

JOHN: No, not really.

DAD: And you probably felt you were being dumped
on and it was unfair?

JOHN: Yeah. You bet.

DAD: Well, since there was nothing you could do, I
wonder what might happen if you give it permission to have happened and just go with it?

JOHN: What?! How would that help? That is worse
than what I did!

DAD: Well, you could say to yourself, "This isn't
what I wanted to happen, but it has. And I don't
want it to upset me so much, so I'll go with it.
I'll just say it's unfortunate, but I can accept it. I
can handle the disappointment. In fact, I'll even
give it permission to happen." If you said that,
you'd be more in control of what was happening
and how you were feeling. It's just a thought.
You may want to use it sometime.

This works! I have seen it work in countless situations—with adults and with teens. We can't apply it to everything that happens, but we can to a lot of things. Have you ever given yourself permission to be stuck in traffic, to be late for an appointment, or to flub the lines when you're talking? Try it. The inner response certainly will be less stressful than fighting the problem.

Ways to Help

There are three approaches you could use to help your teen handle his stress. Two of the ways offer only temporary help or no help at all. The third is the best.

First, you could encourage him to change his environment in order to prevent things that are likely to produce stress. This might include changing part-time jobs, changing friends, church, school, time spent with step-parents, etc. Unfortunately, most people do not realize how many additional changes would be involved with each of the above, and those could create even more stress. Not a very good method.

The second approach would be to teach your teen to recognize and do something about the symptoms. Any of us can attempt to alter our emotional and physiological responses to stress by using medication, tranquilizers, relaxation techniques, meditation or imagery. Not a very good method either.

Here is the third approach to helping a teen handle stress, and I'm sure you will agree it is the best way. It is: Help him learn to alter his assumptions and negative ways of thinking. These are what make him more vulnerable to stress.

Along with showing them alternate ways of interpreting life's frustrations, what other things can parents do to help their teens handle stress? Many times we can't change their environment or the other pressures of their lives outside the home, but we can assist them in their efforts to develop coping skills. And within the family we can make the changes necessary to ensure a positive environment.

Establishing Rules

One of the best ways to assist a teen is to help him distinguish between what he wants and what he needs. It is often helpful to a teen for an adult to say no. Parents have that right. It may mean a confrontation or bucking peer pressure, but those actions are sometimes necessary.

Remember, any rule you make must be enforceable. Here are two guidelines to follow in establishing rules with a teen:

1. *Share with him the principle behind the rule.*

Saying he doesn't need to know the reason does little to help him think—to consider the pros and cons of what he wants to do versus what you want him to do.

2. *Enlist your teen's help in establishing the rule when it is appropriate.*

We did this years ago just prior to our daughter's learning to drive. Here is what all three of us came up with at a family council meeting:

DRIVING AGREEMENT

1. Before using either car, I will ask my mom or dad if I can use it and explain the purpose.
2. If I want to go somewhere for myself, my homework and piano practicing must be completed first.
3. During the first six months of driving with my own license, I will not use the radio while driving.

4. During the school year, I will be allowed to drive to church on Wednesday nights but cannot take anyone home without prior permission.

5. I will not allow anyone else to use the car under any circumstances.

6. I will be allowed up to thirty-five miles a week and after that I must pay for any additional mileage.

7. I will not carry more than five passengers at any time in the Plymouth nor more than three in the Audi.

8. Upon receiving my driver's permit I will be allowed to drive to church and run local errands when either Mom or Dad is along. I will assist in driving for extended periods of time or on long vacations under all types of driving conditions.

9. I will not give rides to hitchhikers under any conditions nor will I accept a ride if I should have any difficulty with the car.

10. I will either wash the car myself or have it done once every three weeks.

11. I will pay half the increase of the insurance costs and in case of an accident I will assume half the deductible cost.

Handling Type A Stress

Think back with me to the three kinds of stress described earlier—Types A, B and C. Remember that Type A is foreseeable and avoidable. Even though teens may be aware of what's coming, they still tend to worry about how to actually handle the situation. Hear some of their concerns:

"How do I prepare for that crazy midterm exam?"

"How do I turn down that dull job my uncle is offering me?"

"I just know Jeff is going to ask me to

the prom. He's nice as a friend, but I'm hoping Jim will ask me. How do I turn Jeff down without hurting him?"

If you were the teen's parent, what would you say? Would you make suggestions? Tell him or her what to do? Or draw out of your teen his own ideas?

Why not suggest a plan he could implement when you're not around? Here is a simple approach involving only three steps:

1. Identify the stress. For a teen, this is probably the easiest of these three steps.

2. Explore your options. This is usually the most difficult.

3. Take the necessary action. Sometimes easy, sometimes not.

For example, you might encourage your teen to brainstorm aloud his options for handling the job offer from his uncle. He could:

— Just not respond and avoid (bad choice).

— Ask Mom or Dad to turn it down for him (another bad choice).

— Take the job out of obligation and tough it out (still a bad choice since it does not teach him how to confront a problem honestly — nor do the preceding two).

— Say to the uncle, "Thank you for the offer. I've considered it but have decided I won't be taking the job. It doesn't really fit the direction I'm going. I'm disappointed that I won't be with you as much as I wanted."

The Broken-Record Technique

As for the date invitation, the less said the better when turning it down. The more reasons a teen gives, the more control she gives the person asking and the more she weakens her own position. A response to a date invitation could be, "I'm sorry, but I'm unable to go with you that evening." If the person asks why not, the teen can answer with the same response: "I'm sorry, but I am unable to go with you that night."

If invited to use alcohol or drugs, a simple response is sufficient, such as, "No, thanks. I don't use that—and I don't want to try it."

No matter what kind of statements or pressure tactics others use, if the teen simply repeats his statement over and over, he will stay in control. This is called the broken-record technique. It involves *not* telling "why." We have the freedom not to give our reasons. By doing this, a teen will have more resistance to the peer group.

Encourage your teen to work out the problem by himself. If you take over a teen's responsibilities, you delay his experiences of becoming an adult. Help him stand on his own and make his own decisions.

Handling Types B and C Stress

Learning to handle the difficulties of Type B stress, the unforeseeable and unavoidable, will be a lifelong process. The best way to help your teen is:

1. Understand the normal phases a person goes through in a crisis.
2. Develop a biblical perspective on life's crises yourself.
3. Begin to share this information with your teen

as early in his life as possible. How? Read *How to Have a Creative Crisis* by this author.[1] You and your teen could read that book — along with this one — together.

I like what Chuck Swindoll says about crisis:

> Crisis crushes. And in crushing, it often refines and purifies. You may be discouraged today because the crushing has not yet led to a surrender. However, I've stood beside too many of the dying, ministered to too many of the broken and bruised to believe that crushing is an end in itself. Unfortunately, it usually takes the brutal blows of affliction to soften and penetrate hard hearts, though such blows often seem unfair. . . . After crises crush sufficiently, God steps in to comfort and teach.[2]

Many of the Type C stresses, the foreseeable but unavoidable, occur because of what a person has to do. This is where developing good problem-solving skills will make a difference.[3]

How can you assist your teen in handling Type C stress? First of all, what does he see in you? Do we as parents reflect a positive model in handling our own daily frustrations?

Four-Step Problem Solving

Let me suggest a very simple method of problem-solving you can share with your teen. Some basic questions are involved in this four-step process:

FOUR-STEP PROBLEM SOLVING PROCESS

Step 1 — What is my problem?

Your teen is faced with the problem of studying for an important midterm exam, the results of which are vital for college entrance. Then he receives an invitation to go, at the same time, with a friend who won an all-expense-paid weekend ski trip for two.

Step 2 — How can this be solved?
What are my alternatives?

Choice one and the consequences: The teen can go on the ski trip, which probably would never occur again because of the unique circumstances. The consequences are quite obvious — not being prepared for the exam and perhaps not having the grades for college.

Choice two: Stay home and study for the exam and perhaps have a chance for college (that is, if he can keep his mind on studying and not mope about missing the trip).

Choice three: Study as much as possible before and on the trip. This would necessitate letting the friend know how important the studying is. It could also involve studying in the car and perhaps isolating himself at times in order to study. Question: Has the teen ever done this before, and is it worth the risk? Does he have the self-discipline to do it?

Step 3 — What is my plan for solving this?

The teen will need to make a choice and then come up with a detailed plan (in writing) in order to follow through. Believe it or not, there are some teens who could carry out this choice.

Step 4 — What will the results be?

It is important to both *anticipate* the results of a choice and then *evaluate* the actual results afterward. To help the teen project possible results, ask him questions like, "If you did that, what do you think would be the result?" Or, "What have you tried before, and what's something new that you haven't thought of yet that would bring different results?" Or, "What else might you try?" And, "What could you do then?"[4]

Helping your teen become aware of his options will help him handle and lessen the stresses in his life.

Building Your Teen's Self-Esteem

Your teen was not born with his (or her) self-concept but it has been in the process of formation for years. As others approved or disapproved of him, he developed an inner opinion of himself. For example, if a child grows up with a critical parent, he may incorporate that parent's attitude within himself and then respond to himself in that same critical way for the rest of his life.

It may not help now to say that the emphasis on self-esteem and identity formation should have begun at a very early age, but it is true. Nor will it help to blame ourselves—we are all amateur parents. What is important is what we can do now for our teens and for our younger children.

No matter how we responded to our children when they were younger, they need our verbal and nonverbal expressions of love and acceptance today. They need to be touched; *they need to be listened to.* Our listening conveys the message that they are valued, that they have something worthwhile to say. It also means you are not judging what is being said nor how it is being said. It means you can feed back to your teen what you have heard him say and how he is feeling. Does that sound like a big task? Perhaps it is, but it is necessary in *all* types of relationships.

Consider these questions about your own teen:

- How does he feel about himself?
- When does she feel good about herself?
- When does he feel down on himself?
- What are her values?
- What is important to him?
- What does she do to value herself?
- Has he learned self-assertion skills to handle peer pressure?

Have you asked your teen these questions? Have you asked in a way that will draw out answers? Discussing those answers with your teen will help him develop a more positive self-concept.

In addition to the above, you can *help him identify and accept his strengths and weaknesses.* How do you do that? Here's one way.

Suggest that your teen *and you* each list your own strengths and weaknesses, and then share them. Show him how you feel about the items on your list and what you might do to strengthen your weaknesses. Then see if your teen is willing to share his list. Be sure to listen, listen, listen! Do not judge him, and do not attempt to fix problems for him. Questions like, "What have you thought about trying?" may draw out some of his own problem-solving ability and help him use it.

Are you thinking, *Why should I write and share my own list?* Well, why not? Your teen needs your openness, vulnerability and modeling in order for him to grow and develop. Besides, you may be amazed at what you learn about yourself!

Encourage your teen. In 1 Thessalonians 5:11 we read: "Encourage . . . and build up one another." Believe in your teen. Help him set reasonable goals and plans, and then stand by him and let him know you are praying for him. Praise your teen and encourage him to develop a sense of pride in his accomplishments. Enjoy what he has both done and experienced, but help him to understand he does not have to become adequate through performance to gain importance in the sight of God. Rather, he has been given authentic value through what God has done for him in the gift of His Son.

Help your teen learn to:

● enjoy his own company

● listen to his own thoughts and feelings; and

● value who he is.

Reinforce him as a person so he can respect who he is and who he thinks he is. This is an excellent preventive when teens face peer pressure to conform.

Here are some positive beliefs you can share with your teen. You may want to ask him to evaluate each of these beliefs on a scale of 1 to 10 to see how strong or weak each belief is at this time.

EVALUATE YOUR BELIEFS

Positive, Healthy and Balanced Beliefs

● It is NOT necessary to be liked by everyone.

● I do NOT have to earn anyone's approval or acceptance to be a person of worth.

● I am a child of God. I'm deeply loved by Him, and I have been forgiven by Him; therefore, I am acceptable. I accept myself.

● My needs and wants are as important as other people's.

- Rejection is NOT terrible. It may be a bit unpleasant, but it is not terrible.

- Not being approved of or accepted by other people is NOT terrible. It may not be desirable, but it is not terrible.

- If somebody doesn't like me, I can live with it. I don't have to work feverishly to get him or her to like me.

- I can conquer my bad feelings by distinguishing the truth from misbelief.

- It is a misbelief that I must please other people and be approved by them.

- Jesus died on a cross for me so I can be free from the misbelief that other people decide my value.

A strong belief in these principles is vital, and repeating them to himself will be the best input a teen can get. It will do a great deal toward helping him develop a positive self-concept and thus be able to cope effectively with the stresses in his life.

The Word of God

Another way to help your teen is by showing him how to apply the Scriptures to life's upsets. Memorizing the Word of God and understanding both the meaning of the Scripture and how to apply it gives stability. One very helpful passage is James 1:2,3:

Consider it all joy, my brethren, when you encounter various trials, knowing that the testing [or trying] of your faith produces endurance.

The word *consider,* or count, actually means an internal attitude of the heart or mind that determines whether the trials and circumstances of life will affect us adversely or beneficially. Another way James 1:2 can be translated is: "Make up your mind to regard adversity as something to welcome or be glad about."

Each of us has the ability to decide what our attitude will be. We can approach a frustrating situation or a tragedy and say, "That's terrible. It's totally upsetting. That is the last thing I wanted to have happen. Why me, and why now?"

Or we can say, "It's not what I wanted, but it's here. I am disappointed and wish it hadn't turned out this way, but it did, so how can I make the best of it?"

It doesn't mean we won't experience pain, or disappointment, or an initial sense of frustration. We cannot deny that, but we can ask, "What can I learn from this? How can I respond to it so it doesn't control me or keep me from moving ahead with my life?"

There may be moments when a teen's responses to things that have happened seem totally negative. At these times we may have to remind him that he can choose to say, "I think there is a better way of responding to this. I want to see this from another perspective." God created all of us with the capacity to learn to respond this way. Ultimately, a person's view of God and of theology will affect how he or she handles a stress-producing crisis or situation.

We cannot insulate and protect our teens against the difficult times and stresses of life—and it is good that we can't. We would be doing them a disservice. Life IS difficult! Life is full of pressures and trials, but there is something we can do. We can assist our teens to learn—at an earlier age than many of us learned—how to face and handle stress through the resources provided by God. The opportunity to develop these skills at an earlier age will give our teens greater stability.

When a teen experiences stress, it can have one of two influences on his relationship with God the same as when an adult is under stress. It can draw the teen closer, or it can cause him to turn away in bitterness and frustration. Isaiah 43:2 is an understanding and realistic description of stress, and it contains a promise:

> When you pass through the waters, I will be with you; and through the rivers, they will not overflow you. When you walk through the fire, you will not be scorched, nor will the flame burn you.

None of us is promised a life free of difficult situations, but we do have the promise that we are not alone when those things arise.

Our stability—and our teen's stability—comes from Christ Himself. He is our strength when we endeavor to help a teen in stress and crisis, and He is that teen's strength as well.

> Now to Him *who is able to establish you* according to my gospel and the preaching of Jesus Christ, according to the revelation of the mystery which has been kept secret for long ages past . . . (Romans 16:25, italics mine).

> Then he said to them, "Go, eat of the fat, drink of the sweet, and send portions to him who has nothing prepared; for this day is holy to our Lord. Do not be grieved, for the *joy of the LORD is your strength*" (Nehemiah 8:10, italics mine).

> And He shall be the *stability of your times,* a wealth of salvation, wisdom, and knowledge; the fear of the LORD is his treasure (Isaiah 33:6, italics mine).

APPENDIX

TEEN STRESS PROFILE

One of the best ways to help a teen cope with stress is to help him (or her) determine the degree of stress in his life. Below is a "Teen Scene Stress Test" you can give your teen.

One suggestion: Never use the word *test* to your teen, especially if you plan this on a weekend. *Inventory* or *profile* is a good substitute.

Before you suggest he do this, take a separate piece of paper and, relating the questions to your teen, answer them yourself from your own perspective as you have watched him handle stress. After he has completed the profile, let him know that you did it, too, from your observations of his handling stress and, if he's interested, you would be glad to share the results with him.

This quiz will enable you and your teenager to determine both the level of stress in his life right now and how well he handles it.

Your youngster should keep his answers just as honest and accurate as possible. If he is afraid to complete the profile or belligerently refuses to do so, encourage him in terms that he can understand and appreciate. Your teen needs you to point out that doing this inventory will put him more in touch with his own feelings and will help him understand why sometimes he seems "out of it."

When your teen has finished, score the results and go through an explanation of the score with him. Then let him go back to his records and tapes while you review the test once more yourself. Did you predict your child's answers accurately? Do you know him as well as you thought? Don't be surprised if your answer to both of these questions is no. This profile is designed to help you better understand your child, the stress he is going through, and how you can help lessen it.

TEEN SCENE STRESS TEST

	OFTEN	SOMETIMES	SELDOM	NEVER
1. During the past three months, have you been under considerable strain, stress, or pressure?	—	—	—	—
2. Have you experienced any of the following symptoms: palpitations or a racing heart, dizziness, blushing, painfully cold hands or feet, shallow or fast breathing, nail biting, restless body or legs, butterflies in stomach, insomnia, chronic fatigue?	—	—	—	—
3. In general, do you have headaches or digestive upsets?	—	—	—	—

4. Do you have crying spells
   or feel like crying?   __ __ __ __

5. Do you have recurring
   nightmares?   __ __ __ __

6. Do you have pain in your neck,
   back, or arms?   __ __ __ __

7. Do you feel depressed or
   unhappy?   __ __ __ __

8. Do you worry excessively?   __ __ __ __

9. Do you ever feel anxious even
   though you don't know why?   __ __ __ __

10. Are you ever edgy or impatient
    with your parents or other
    family members?   __ __ __ __

11. Are you ever overwhelmed
    by hopelessness?   __ __ __ __

12. Do you dwell on things you
    should have done but didn't?   __ __ __ __

13. Do you dwell on things you
    did but shouldn't have?   __ __ __ __

14. Do you have any problems
    focusing on your schoolwork?   __ __ __ __

15. When you're criticized, do you
    brood about it?   __ __ __ __

16. Do you worry about what
    others think?   __ __ __ __

17. Are you bored?   __ __ __ __

18. Do you feel envy or resentment
    when someone has something
    you don't have?   __ __ __ __

19. Do you quarrel with your
    boyfriend/girlfriend?   __ __ __ __

20. Are there serious conflicts
    between your parents?   __ __ __ __

	YES	NO
21. Lately, do you find yourself more irritable and argumentative than usual?	—	—
22. Are you as popular with friends as you'd wish?	—	—
23. Are you doing as well in school as you'd like?	—	—
24. Do you feel you can live up to your parents' expectations?	—	—
25. Do you feel that your parents understand your problems and are supportive?	—	—
26. On the whole, are you satisfied with the way you look?	—	—
27. Do you have trouble with your teachers?	—	—
28. Do you sometimes worry that your friends might be turning against you?	—	—
29. Do you have enough spending money to cover your needs?	—	—
30. Have you noticed lately that you eat, drink or smoke more than you really should?	—	—
31. Do you make strong demands on yourself?	—	—
32. Do you feel the limits imposed by your parents regarding what you may or may not do are justified?	—	—
33. Do your parents always criticize you?	—	—
34. Do you have any serious worries concerning your love relationships with the opposite sex?	—	—
35. Are any of your brothers or sisters overly competitive with you?	—	—
36. Do you feel left out of social gatherings?	—	—
37. Do you habitually fall behind in your schoolwork?	—	—
38. Do you feel tense and defensive when you're around someone your age of the		

      opposite sex?   —   —

39. Have you, or has anyone in your family, suffered a severe illness or injury in the last year?   —   —

40. Do you experience any conflict between your own standards and peer pressure to engage in certain activities?   —   —

41. Have you recently moved to a new home, school or community?   —   —

42. Have you been rejected by a boyfriend/girlfriend within the last three months?   —   —

43. Is it very difficult for you to say no to requests?   —   —

44. Have your grades taken a sudden drop lately?   —   —

45. Do you often become ill after an emotional upset?   —   —

<u>Scoring</u>: Add up your points based on this answer key:

	(a)	(b)	(c)	(d)		(a)	(b)	(c)	(d)
1.	7	4	1	0	11.	7	3	1	0
2.	7	4	I	0	12.	4	2	0	0
3.	6	3	1	0	13.	4	2	0	0
4.	5	2	1	0	14.	4	2	0	0
5.	6	3	1	0	15.	4	2	0	0
6.	4	2	0	0	16.	4	2	0	0
7.	7	3	1	0	17.	4	2	0	0
8.	6	3	1	0	18.	4	2	0	0
9.	6	3	1	0	19.	5	3	1	0
10.	5	2	0	0	20.	5	3	1	0

	Yes	No		Yes	No		Yes	No
21.	4	0	30.	5	0	38.	3	0
22.	0	3	31.	4	0	39.	6	0
23.	0	4	32.	0	3	40.	5	0
24.	0	5	33.	4	0	41.	3	0
25.	0	5	34.	5	0	42.	4	0
26.	0	4	35.	3	0	43.	3	0
27.	3	0	36.	4	0	44.	4	0
28.	4	0	37.	3	0	45.	5	0
29.	0	3						

WHAT YOUR SCORE MEANS

116-203. A score in this range indicates that your troubles outnumber your satisfactions and that you are currently subjected to a high level of stress. No doubt, you are already aware of your problems and are rightfully concerned.

You should do everything possible to avoid as many tense situations as you can until you feel more in control of your life. Review the quiz to pinpoint the major sources of your stress. Try to develop more effective ways of dealing with difficult human relationships and circumstances. Perhaps you are overreacting to problems or are not as willing to cope as you could be. Think about getting some kind of professional help. Sometimes even a few hours of counseling can be beneficial.

62-115. A score spanning this range signifies that the level of stress in your life is moderate, or that you are handling your frustrations quite well. However, because you have occasional difficulty managing the effects of stress, consider some new methods of overcoming disappointments. Remember, we all have to face and live with frustrations and anxieties.

0-61. A score in this range points to a relatively low stress level. In spite of minor worries and concerns, you are not in any serious trouble. You have good adaptive powers and are able to deal successfully with situations that make you temporarily uptight.[1]

NOTES

Chapter 1

1. Bettie B. Youngs, *Helping Your Teenager Deal With Stress* (Los Angeles, CA: Jeremy P. Tarcher, 1986), p. 66. Adapted.

Chapter 2

1. Donald C. Meadows, Barbara J. Porter and I. David Welch, *Children Under Stress* (Englewood Cliffs, NJ: Prentice-Hall, 1983), pp. 10-12.

2. Dr. Bettie B. Youngs, *Stress in Children* (New York: Avon Books, 1985), pp. 55-57. Adapted.

3. The survey, done by *Children and Teens Today* magazine, appeared in *Marriage and Divorce* 11:51 (July 21, 1986), n.p., from which we have quoted.

4. Mary Susan Miller, *Childstress* (Garden City, NY: Doubleday & Co., Inc., 1982), pp. 22-23.

5. Miller, *Childstress,* pp. 26-33. Adapted.

6. Meadows, *Children,* pp. 11-12.

Chapter 3

1. H. Norman Wright, *How to Have a Creative Crisis* (Waco, TX: Word Books, 1987).

2. David Eskind, *All Grown Up and No Place to Go* (Menlo Park, CA: Addison Wesley, 1982), pp. 168-77. Adapted.

3. Keith W. Sehnert, *Stress/Unstress* (Minneapolis: Augsburg, 1981), pp. 74-75. Adapted.

Chapter 4

1. G. Keith Olson, *Counseling Teenagers* (Loveland, CO: Group Books, 1984), pp. 36-37.

2. Antionette Saunders and Bonnie Remsberg, *The Stress-Proof Child* (New York: New American Library, 1984), pp. 31-32. Adapted.

3. Bettie B. Youngs, *Helping Your Teenager Deal With Stress* (Los Angeles: Jeremy P. Tarcher, 1986), pp. 95-97. Adapted.

Chapter 5

1. Jonathan Kellerman, *Helping the Fearful Child* (New York: W. W. Norton & Co., Inc., 1986).

Chapter 6

1. Brent Q. Hofen and Brenda Peterson, *The Crisis Intervention Handbook* (Englewood Cliffs, NJ: Prentice-Hall, 1982), pp. 21-39. Adapted.

2. E. Lindemann, "Symptometology and Management of Acute Grief," *American Journal of Psychiatry* (1981), 139:141-48.

3. G. Keith Olson, *Counseling Teenagers* (Loveland, CO: Group Books, 1984), pp. 27-28.

4. Frederick F. Flach and Suzanne C. Draughi, *The Nature and Treatment of Depression* (New York: Wiley, 1975), pp. 104-6. Adapted.

5. Bettie B. Youngs, *Helping Your Teenager Deal With Stress* (Los Anageles: Jeremy P. Tarcher, Inc., 1986), pp. 180-81. Adapted.

Chapter 7

1. Archibald Hart, *Children and Divorce: What to Expect and How to Help* (Waco, TX: Word Publishers, 1982), pp. 124-25.

2. *Marriage and Divorce Today* (May 18, 1987), 12:42, n.p.

3. H. Norman Wright, *Always Daddy's Girl* (Ventura, CA: Regal Books, n.d.).

4. H. Norman Wright, *Crisis Counseling* (San Bernardino, CA: Here's Life Publishers, 1986), pp. 167-172. Adapted.

Chapter 8

1. Tim Hansel, *When I Relax I Feel Guilty* (Elgin, IL: David C. Cook, 1979).

2. Dave and Jan Congo, *Less Stress* (Ventura, CA: Regal, n.d.).

3. H. Norman Wright, *How to Have a Creative Crisis* (Waco, TX: Word Books, 1987).

4. Mary Susan Miller, *Childstress* (Garden City, NY: Doubleday & Co., Inc., 1982), pp. 42-53. Adapted.

Chapter 9

1. H. Norman Wright, *How to Have a Creative Crisis* (Waco, TX: Word Books, 1987).

2. Charles R. Swindoll, *Growing Strong in the Seasons of Life* (Portland, OR: Multnomah Press, 1983), pp. 274-75.

3. David Eskind, *All Grown Up and No Place to Go* (Menlo Park, CA: Addison Wesley, 1982), pp. 200-214. Adapted.

4. Eskind, *All Grown Up*, pp. 200-214. Adapted.

Appendix

1. Bettie B. Youngs, *Helping Your Teenager Deal With Stress* (Los Angeles: Jeremy P. Tarcher, 1986), pp. 13-17.

Helping Your Kids
Through Adolescence

Quantity   Total

_____ **MOM AND DAD DON'T LIVE TOGETHER ANYMORE** *by* $ _____
Gary & Angela Hunt. Help and encouragement for youth and
their parents who are working through the confusing time of
separation or divorce. ISBN 0-89840-199-2/$5.95

_____ **NOW THAT HE'S ASKED YOU OUT** *by Gary & Angela* $ _____
Hunt. Straight talk for junior high girls . . . Focuses on key
dating issues including: when she is old enough to date, what
mature, Christian young men look for in a date and what role
parents can play. ISBN 0-89840-258-1/$6.95

_____ **NOW THAT YOU'VE ASKED HER OUT** *by Gary & Angela* $ _____
Hunt. Straight talk for junior high guys . . . Answers questions
about when he is ready to date, curfews and dating guidelines,
and relates facts about AIDS, teen pregnancy and abortion.
ISBN 0-89840-259-X/$6.95

_____ **WHY TEENS ARE KILLING THEMSELVES: AND WHAT** $ _____
WE CAN DO ABOUT IT *by Marion Duckworth.* This book ex-
plains why teens turn to suicide and what the home, church and
community can do to prevent it. ISBN 0-89840-169-0/$8.95

_____ **SURVIVING THE TWEENAGE YEARS** *by Gary & Angela* $ _____
Hunt. Walks parents and youth workers through the contradictory maze of preteen and early teen reactions to emotional,
physical and mental changes in their lives.
ISBN 0-89840-205-0/$6.95

Indicate product(s) desired above. Fill out below.
Send to:

HERE'S LIFE PUBLISHERS, INC.	**ORDER TOTAL** $ _____
P. O. Box 1576	SHIPPING and
San Bernardino, CA 92402-1576	HANDLING $ _____
	($1.50 for one book,
NAME_____	$0.50 for each additional.
	Do not exceed $4.00.)
ADDRESS_____	APPLICABLE
	SALES TAX (CA, 6%)$ _____
STATE_____ZIP_____	**TOTAL DUE** $ _____

PAYABLE IN U.S. FUNDS.
☐ Payment (check or money order only) (No cash orders accepted.)
   included
☐ Visa   ☐ Mastercard #_____

Expiration Date_____Signature_____

**FOR FASTER SERVICE
CALL TOLL FREE:
1-800-950-4457**   Also ordering other side ☐   HKH 271-9

BUILDING BETTER FAMILIES

Practical Resources
to Strengthen Your Home

Quantity   Total

____ **PULLING WEEDS, PLANTING SEEDS: Grow-** $____
ing Character in Your Life and Family *by Den-*
nis Rainey. An inspiring collection of pointed
reflections on personal and family life with an abundance of practical insights for everyday living.
ISBN 0-89840-217-4/hardcover, $12.95

____ **THE DAD DIFFERENCE: Creating an En-** $____
vironment for Your Child's Sexual Wholeness
by Josh McDowell and Dr. Norm Wakefield. Sets
the stage for fathering that will dramatically im-
prove parent/teen relationships and reduce teen
sexual excesses. Practical examples of role modeling
and father/children activities.
ISBN 0-89840-252-2/$8.95

____ **PARENTING SOLO** *by Dr. Emil Authelet.* Take $____
the fear—and some of the frustration—out of single
parenting. Helpful ideas for laying a strong biblical
foundation, understanding your need for healing,
and overcoming barriers that keep you and your
children from growing and enjoying a fulfilling life.
ISBN 0-89840-197-6/$7.95

Indicate product(s) desired above. Fill out below.
Send to:

HERE'S LIFE PUBLISHERS, INC. P. O. Box 1576 San Bernardino, CA 92402-1576	**ORDER TOTAL** $____
	SHIPPING and HANDLING $____ ($1.50 for one book, $0.50 for each additional. Do not exceed $4.00.)
NAME_____	
ADDRESS_____	APPLICABLE SALES TAX (CA, 6%) $____
STATE_____ZIP_____	**TOTAL DUE** $____
	PAYABLE IN U.S. FUNDS. (No cash orders accepted.)
☐ Payment (check or money order only) included	

☐ Visa   ☐ Mastercard #_____

Expiration Date_____Signature_____

FOR FASTER SERVICE
CALL TOLL FREE:
1-800-950-4457   Also ordering other side ☐   HKH 271-9